Red Sky

poetry on the global epidemic of violence against women

edited by
melissa hassard
gabrielle langley
stacy nigliazzo

Cover and interior design by Sable Books

ISBN 978-0-9968036-6-3

Library of Congress Control Number: 2016915393

Printed in USA

Sable Books
sablebooks.org

for every woman under the sky

Contents

Introduction

On May 21, 2015, in Houston, Texas, a woman was stabbed to death in her own home by her estranged boyfriend. Her name was Caroline Minjares. She worked as an emergency room nurse, together with one of the editors of this anthology, Stacy Nigliazzo. Stacy remembers Caroline as:

> ...a young mother with thoughtful eyes and long brown hair. The last time I saw her was just after a fall sunrise, at shift-change. She had a beautiful smile, even after twelve hours overnight on the unit...

In response to the murder of Caroline Minjares, the following headlines appeared:

> *Houston firefighter dies in apparent murder-suicide*
> (Reuters)

> *Houston firefighter found dead in Northeast Houston home*
> (City of Houston media alert)

> *Texas Firefighter Richard Deluna kills girlfriend in murder-suicide*
> (Daily Mail)

Bizarrely, the name and profession of Caroline's murderer made all the headlines, while her own name did not.

Stacy sent the following email (in part) to KHOU (a Houston news outlet):

> ...A woman was murdered in your city last night—her name was Caroline Minjares—and your story begins as follows: *A Houston firefighter has died in an apparent murder-suicide.* The very least you could do is mention her name in the headline, or perhaps even lead with *Houston nurse* instead of *Houston firefighter.* Let's be clear about who the victim is, here. I seriously doubt she slit her own throat...

Still in shock, and angry, Stacy used these news reports to craft an erasure poem in honor of Caroline's memory. A few days later, she completed her initial draft, sending it to Gabrielle Langley for review. (Coincidentally, Stacy and Gabrielle had sat together at a poetry reading in a Houston coffee house on the same night that Stacy would learn of Caroline's death.) These two Houston poets began discussing an idea for an anthology where poets could address issues of violence against women.

Shortly after Stacy's poem for Caroline was finished, it was published by Lumen Magazine. Providentially, Melissa Hassard of Sable Books read the poem and promptly contacted Stacy. Melissa also had the idea and hope of organizing an anthology of poetry addressing violence against women. Weaving together her resources and publishing experience through Sable Books, Melissa Hassard, in effect, waved the magic wand that was needed, ensuring that a project of this scope could be organized, printed and distributed. Within that same week, Melissa Hassard, Gabrielle Langley, and Stacy Nigliazzo were on a conference call

and this book was born.

This anthology was born from the death of one woman. However, as anyone who pays even casual attention to news media is aware, Caroline Minjares' story is only one of countless. Consider the following data made available by the World Health Organization:

- Recent global prevalence figures indicate that about 1 in 3 (35%) of women worldwide have experienced either physical and/or sexual intimate partner violence or non-partner sexual violence in their lifetime.

- Most of this violence is intimate partner violence. Worldwide, almost one-third (30%) of women who have been in a relationship report that they have experienced some form of physical and/or sexual violence by their intimate partner.

- Globally, as many as 38% of murders of women are committed by an intimate partner.

- Factors associated with increased risk of perpetration of violence include low education, child maltreatment or exposure to violence in the family, harmful use of alcohol, attitudes accepting of violence and gender inequality.

- Factors associated with increased risk of experiencing intimate partner and sexual violence include low education, exposure to violence between parents, abuse during childhood, attitudes accepting violence and gender inequality.

- ...primary prevention strategies, such as micro-finance combined with gender equality training and community-based initiatives that address gender inequality and relationship skills, hold promise.

- Situations of conflict, post-conflict and displacement may exacerbate existing violence, such as by intimate partners, and present additional forms of violence against women

With the call for submissions opened, we were honored to receive close to a thousand poems. It has been truly humbling for the three of us to be able to read so many exceptional works, courageously submitted by poets from all over the world. Even before reminding ourselves of the statistical evidence, the extent of the problem became all the more real to us as we reviewed the submissions. While it will never be possible to include every woman's story in a single anthology, we have done our best to represent the problem from the perspective of poets. We are proud to present a collection of work by established and widely published poets, as well as those who are less well known.

We also knew, from the very beginning of our project, that we wanted to include men's voices as well as women's. As the men's poems in this anthology will attest to, men are also traumatized and diminished by the violence that is, has been, and continues to be committed against women. This violence is threatening the same women who these men love and rely upon. The victims are their mothers, their daughters, their significant others, their sisters, their friends and their colleagues. For this reason, we are very proud to have the voices of women and men speaking together within these pages.

Lest we lose perspective, it is important to acknowledge the growing evidence that our world is, on average, slowly but surely becoming a safer place for women as well as men. With the advancement of Internet technologies and the speed at which we now gather our news, we know that these findings may come as a surprise. Even with the gains, however, there is still much to be done. We must continue the fight against the global oppression of women, even as we celebrate the growing list of battles won. There will always be those who ask us, "What is wrong with you women? With all your advancement and equality, why can't you all just get over it?"

In response to the question of why we women can't "just get over it," we can only conclude that anyone – male or female – who suggests that a victim "just get over it" is, sadly, exhibiting far more concern about their own sense of discomfort than they are about the comfort, safety, and well-being of the victim. Victims begin to heal when they are able to tell their stories. By providing a safe space for the victim to express herself, we support her healing. And while we must acknowledge that the subject matter of these poems will, undoubtedly, take our readers into some very dark and terrifying places, we stand firm in the knowledge that holding this darkness and terror up to the light is the only way we can begin to break its hold.

"What would happen if one woman told the truth about her life?
The world would split open."

— Muriel Rukeyser

Fire on the Prophet's Face

A weightless child thrashes limbs
too small to be felt
                    in the small lake of a mother.

Fur shivers on a coupling fox,
and a bowl of fire lights the prophet's face
                    in a branch-hidden cavern.

Banyan roots tunnel.
Potato fists unfold
                    in mute loam.

A tumor blooms in a skull.
The button-click is quiet in the quiet room,
                    quiet the signal to the unmanned drone.

Words of revolution
swirl through shisha smoke in coffee shops
                    as teaspoons clink and stir.

In the middle of earth fire burns and burns.

                                        Andy Young

Everything Changes the World

Boys on a beach,
women with cookpots,
men bombing tender patches of mint.

Is there a righteous position?
Only a place where brown feet
touch the earth.

Maybe you call it yours.
Maybe someone else runs it.
What do you prefer?

We who are far
stagger under the mind blade.
Words, lies.

Every shattered home,
every story worth telling.
Think how much you'd need to say
if that were your kid.

If one of your people
equals hundreds of ours,
what does that say about people?

Naomi Shihab Nye

How to Write About It

Don't make it rhyme; be quiet when you tell it.
Give it no rhythm, don't clothe it in beauty,
just walk into the room of it without knocking.

You could tell it in third person. Like this:
a woman stands in front of a mirror like wallpaper
(she carries bouquets of purple and yellow
that bloom in loneliness).
Talk about why she barely recognizes herself
in that kind of light. How it's not just the way the light falls
on her features, her layers of skin and fat and skeleton;
not just the bruises she blossoms into,
but the way she blends into every room,
though this one is all tint and flatness.
Tell that the room has no windows.

You could also tell it like it happened to you.
Touch it, but let it be sparse: the tile is so cold it feels wet.
The metal edge of the medicine cabinet is bent and sharp.
The sound of the air conditioner is as empty
as a room when the music ends.
Mention that any other sound now
would be as startling as birds taking wing.
You should try to give it some mystery, too,
at least one line only those invited can enter:
say that she maps her own disaster with silence.

Or just walk around her. She won't even notice you're there.
When you leave, you'll leave her standing alone in the mirror,
as naked as when you came in.

You have seen it so many times you know what will happen.
You can say why it happens.
This time, you could save her if you like.

Or you can just tell it, and don't give any reasons.

Chera Hammons

The (Im)Precision of Language

How far the ring-necked dove is
from wringing a dove's neck. The way
a stand of trees can hide a deer

stand, concealing the hunter who
will shoot the deer. The deer, who will
fall in the fall in the fallow field.

Once, someone who was dear to me
threatened me with a deer rifle. Cleaned
it random times, out of season when

he was upset. Said, *I don't want to be
divorced. We can make this work,* while
working the polishing cloth along the metal

barrel of the gun. My blood barreled through
my body when I would see his truck in the drive.
I was never not scared to come home, to fall

asleep, to say the least little thing wrong.
Language became a tricky game where saying
nothing meant everything, where saying everything

meant nothing left to fear. I sang my sorrow song
to anyone who would listen, recognized the panic
of birdsong, the desperation of the killdeer

feigning its broken wing. Anything to lure the predator
from its nest. Its broken wing was strength
of a different kind. I figured showing my weakness

might help me. Someone might understand the bird
of my heart always crashing against the cage
of my ribs, the moth of hidden fear fluttering

to escape from my throat. Once, in my Shakespeare
class I learned that *brace* meant a pair, a brace
of kinsmen, of harlots, of greyhounds,

a brace of warlike brothers. In another time
I stood at the front of the classroom in a chest
brace because my husband had collapsed

the cartilage between my ribs. I couldn't reach
the string on the movie screen and had to ask
for help. I said, *I'm wearing a brace, so I can't*

stretch. I thought of the grimace stretching
across the nurse's face when I said, *I know,*
this sounds like domestic violence. It was an accident,

just goofing around. I wrapped the Velcro belt
around my ribs each morning as he ribbed me
that I should have given up, What was I trying

to prove by staying in a submission hold
until he cracked my ribs? How could I be
so stupid? So stubborn? I didn't know he

was grooming me for greater violence,
the rock thrown at me in the car,
the wedding ring pressed so tight

by his hand holding mine that I bled.
Which brings us back to the dove,
the difference between ringing

and wringing and where language leaves us
when someone controls every word we say,
when we have no one left to talk to.

Shaindel Beers

Breakfast

The orchid ablaze on the dining room table
after the man last night with a gun on campus
Shot a single bullet into the ground outside

Outside next to the building where I teach my students about language
And how to form an argument.
Right now, I am holding a fork instead of a pen

Instead of a gun. The subject of the sentence is me.
A woman eating an egg, a woman writing a poem.
What is the consciousness of the objects we act upon.

Upon my small plate, the yolk breaks open.
The egg, from a local farm. Someone who I don't know
raised this chicken who bore this egg.

Someone who I don't know raised this child.
Last night he wore shorts as the cool April
evening met his skin as he held a gun in his hands.

In the evening a boy was held by what hell and his holding back.
A purple orchid held up by the breakfast table.
A fork resting on an empty plate. The distance between

lives. Someone raised this gun, all its small parts.
Last night, the sliver of the moon met the silver of the handgun
and for a moment the world shimmers.

All the small pieces. Barrel, trigger, bricks, blades of grass
before the exhale of a bullet, the punctuation of a bullet.
A shot shimmering into silence.

The silence of the ground outside the building where I teach,
After the man last night with a gun used the language
of a gun in an argument in which he is the subject

and the object of a violence held both
too close and so far from the violet blossoms
on the table of a woman eating breakfast.

Carly Sachs

Hibakusha
for Margie Hunt

Sixty years sat like stones on my chest
Pinned me to the surface of the earth

Let me walk and move and talk
As if I went on living after that day

As though I did not see
The burning air, or smell the radiation fires

Containing women, babies strapped to
Their backs; old men playing cards—

That morning I didn't go to my factory job
Instead, I went with Daddy to his

As I sat—daydreaming—head resting on my warm palm
The sky darkened, turned gold, then imploded

The walls around me fell like toothpicks
Scattered on the floor of our restaurant

Afterward, I walked the streets
With my father, searching for my sister

The ground littered with phosphorescent
Flowers glowing like raw embers

Upon closer inspection, I saw pieces of
Skin and bone, not flowers:

A woman's severed hand,
An ear torn from its socket.

Even as my hair fell out in shanks
I did not cry

Even as my father died of brain cancer
My eyes had no water

Even as my mother bled to death
From one slight bruise on her arm

No rain fell on my cheek
I held my breath, bit my tongue

Until six decades
Left me gulping for air

As one small child,
His black hair cut in the shape

Of a noodle bowl, gifted me
With a strand of flame-colored cranes

So I might begin to remember
This clear river inside of me

And finally loosen the broken
Songbird in my throat

Shavawn M. Berry

Relief

"Artists and map makers call [the] ups and downs of surface its relief. Ups and downs, as anyone who has done any walking knows, alter distances. These physical features of an area, natural and manmade, are called its topography."

— from *Mapping,* by David Greenhood

A lover showed me pictures of her belly's stretch marks
and their likeness she found twinned on a tree just outside
her window. I imagined those cyphers curved across her skin
like the tattoo a pocketknife leaves as it angles through the soft

or hard of wood or that they are what remain after two people facing
a tree's body, peel away bark then carve their initials in its buttery flesh—
imagine them a couplet caged in the open mouth of a heart.

These are some of the markings made on a body, these points that
paint the name of the lover brailed on the bicep of the sailor or the
silhouette child sketched on the scapula of the mother. These are the voluntary
latitudes visible across its surface that makes traversing the land—

scape of another less quest and more homecoming. But what of
the markings in? The arbitrary landing of longitude or an inking
that settles in the soil at surface, rises to relief— leaves a topography

of depression? See, there are so many ways people are made map
by moments. The contours creased in the horizontal plane of her cheek.
The creek cut from the curve of his knife on her neck. The cave flooded
by the fingers of a father. All this hatching heaved on the heart by a hand.

Denise Miller

Hands

If not the swallows in the morning then the smell of guano at night permeating her room, emanating from the bridge where protestors ignite vigils the homeless don't mind.

She no more believes the devil each time it appears that it wants her, no more a girl in line for rationed bread admonished by women who say the soldiers have commenced the rapes.

The soldiers knocked and her father said "I'll shoot you if they as much as touch you." She said "If you want to shoot someone shoot yourself."

Fady Joudah

For the Women of Atenco

Take it now, this metaphor, your bread.
You've seen God bleeding in the streets,
but the militia couldn't help, sooty faced
themselves, disoriented by the shrapnel
lodged beneath their right to choose
a peaceful life. Take these words flowing
like wine. Let them salve where hands
gripped too tight, where teeth broke the skin,
where fists beat your notions of freedom
and equality flat as powdered dough, flat
as grapes crushed beneath the pointed
boots of war. Let these words recall
those things you meant to be before
rage came storming through your town.
Let them be your appetizers,
served to you with the humility and respect
you were denied four years ago.
Let these words be your dinners and desserts,
evidence you are being heard. Let them
sustain you, as others sip margaritas on the patio,
as others go on about their lives
oblivious to what you have endured. Your time
will come. So keep your aprons on, women
of Atenco; keep your eyes on the timer
and your hearts on the cause—because grapes
beneath the feet become wine, and
dough that is set aside will rise. Yes—
neglected, resilient dough will rise.

Melissa Studdard

The Last Santa Muerte

You can't imagine the smell rising
among the stacked cardboard boxes
labeled with magic marker—*orejas de raton,*
menta, suelda, mirra—rows of mojo
candles promising fortune, relief
from bad neighbors, skin potions
for the loveless, dust disturbed on tiny
pierced hearts, livers, legs, arms,
Gallo playing cards in the Mexican pattern
with female knaves—as I rummage
the closing sale of the hierbería
deep in the barrio and disinter the last
Santísima Muerte. Bone white,
she cradles scales, a globe in the folds
of her shroud spread over a nest
of seeds. She is patron of the desperate poor,
of the rich drug lords, of all those who pray
for the good death and to stave off
the violent, and of the disappeared,
the women of Juárez whose bodies
are the desert, whose hopes are its wind.

Katherine Durham Oldmixon

From *SWEET/CRUDE: A Bakken Boom Cycle*

VII.

In the man camps, alcohol and drugs make a good social lubricant, smoothing the (high)way for the thousands of roughnecks, petroleum engineers, pipeline catters, truck drivers, carpenters, contractors, and electricians, as well as journalists, adventure scientists, scholars, and photographers who arrive here daily, driven across the continent onto the prairies. *Two Bakken-bound men on meth head out from Montana.* The men outnumber the women by 30%: many leave families swimming in underwater mortgages but otherwise safe as houses, while sex offenders and former inmates unemployable elsewhere also come, wayward past disappeared. *Sherry Arnold, math teacher, heads out for her morning run.*

Oil companies erect dormitory-style barracks, with no tolerance for guns, alcohol, drugs, or women – even spouses. Or RVs and trailers populate amenitied lots with attendant attempts to set boundaries, winterize and hunker down for the long term. Then, there are parked pickups and vans and makeshift shantytowns, frail structures insulated with styrofoam, plywood, and hay or what have you against the cold wind's stinging grit, no water or sewage – the smell carries twelve miles outside of town. *Outside of town, her shoe is found.*

Not enough lubrication, and things break down; but too much is a slippery slope. "We got one guy, got in this other guy's camper and he wouldn't leave, so the guy beat the shit out of him." Concealed-carry permits skyrocket. "We never send just one girl out alone to clean properties, and still they get propositioned." With no set boundaries, reported rapes are up 20%. *A farmer finds her body abandoned in his field.* Glen Crabtree, floor hand at a rig, sports a tattoo reading *Fuck, Fight, or Trip Pipe* and he'll do it, too – he'll ride this boom till it busts.

Heidi Czerwiec

War on Women

September, 2002.
Upon completing basic training, my company commander shared
the following with the women of Bravo Co. 795:
"In this world, you will always be a *bitch* or a *whore*.
Decide now which you prefer they call you."
We'd just learned to maintain and fire M-16s effectively,
but we'd not yet been indoctrinated properly.
As women in the Military Police Corps, she was readying us
for combat. Her words, preparing us for front lines
of a different kind like...

February, 2003.
I'd not yet mastered tactical maneuvers after dinner and drinks,
was ill prepared for the blockading of "NO!" from my mouth.
It wasn't a forceful rape.
More like... an apprehensive surrender.
My exposed skin, white flag. A soft target.
I became easy prey to a Staff Sergeant who'd promised
he'd square me away. This would later include $315,
a drive to and from an abortion clinic,
and a plea not to tell his wife
about what we'd done.

June, 2009.
For refusing the Depo shot offered to deploying female soldiers,
a fellow squad member accused me of trying to get pregnant.
As if I had in mind an EPT's blue plus sign to be my ticket home,
an early trip back from Iraq. As if my choice of birth control
was anybody's business but my own, he stated:
"Well, if bitches can't be trusted to keep their legs closed overseas,
they damn sure can't be trusted to take a pill every day."
I would later pull convoy security alongside him. Drive. Gun.
Work the same checkpoints he did. Search women and children
when he couldn't, ensuring our safety.
Once home, his wife thanked me
for bringing him back
in one piece.

Today.
Planted along capitol steps,
bills against women lie in wait. A daisy chain of trip wires.
Rape redefined. The attempted overturn of Roe v. Wade.
Restrictions on birth control. Minds set. Politicians spew,
"It is unpatriotic to use the phrase 'War on Women!'"
The phrase somehow disrespectful to the soldiers who've served
in a "real war." Their words, rousing the 144 women who've died
while serving in Iraq and Afghanistan, spinning them over in
graves
and unearthing their sacrifice. Listen closely.
You will hear a platoon of ghostly voices question:
"What else should we call this then?"
Because war is a state of hostility.
A struggle between opposing forces.
A hostile conflict with a particular end.
And this is women against
rightwingedConservativereligiousmen.
Them versus us sluts and prostitutes,
who are to lay down,
take it,
roll over,
beg
like the good bitches they've trained us to be,
unable to make decisions concerning our own bodies,
yet able to die unacknowledged
for this country.

It has always started with a name.

Bitch. Whore.
Feminist.
Terrorist.

And I've fought
enough wars to know
labels that strip us
of our humanity
make mass murder
easy.

Casandra Faith Broaddus

After Which We Never Speak to Each Other Again, 1994
after C. K. Williams

Once, near Leipzig, a beautiful boy, fifteen, sixteen maybe, at the station,
    a one-track, one-employee station, with three people waiting,
us and this boy, his face suffused with a light that sat somewhere
    between bone and skin, this boy arched his back, his neck—
red curls cut neat above his combat jacket's collar, snapped his head,
    and spit on us, through pursed pink lips he spit
in our faces, on the platform, in the open, and asked what the fuck
    we were doing there, as if you didn't have a ticket, a *Deutsche*
Bahn ticket you held for him to see, as if I didn't try to say *Her train*
    leaves at 4:30. His spit tasted of beer.
We were young still, women barely, barely knowing each other but
    needing to speak the flat "a" of our mutual vocabulary,
our home language more like well-worn jeans to us than German.
    We forgot to blend in, laughing loudly, cocksure
with Western expansion, of having planted our flag in the dusty,
    pocked surface of the concrete platform. He drew close,
his face in your face as if he meant to kiss you. For a moment, I looked
    away, looked down at his black leather boots scuffing your shoes,
and saw the vulnerable inch of skin between his hem and boot top—
    as if he'd bared himself for us to bandage a wound.

Ashley Nissler

Berlin, May 1945
für Lotte und Louise

Into the ruins
on hob-nail boots
the Russian soldiers
marched
prowled
the rubble
wolf-bristled
foam-mouthed
hunted down
the youngest
the prettiest
made *her* pay
for Hitler
for Stalingrad
for a hundred flowering
linden trees
uprooted
splintered and sold
for firewood
for the wild game
that fled *Tiergarten*
the venison and rabbit
the crack of a rifle
stones cried
battered roses
blackened-red
the Russian boot
his knife
her dress
ripped silk
shredded crepe
the signs
on broken pavement
the stains
soaked into concrete.

Gabrielle Langley

Requiem for a Shark

Watch out for the fat shark's attacks, all fangs out.
Forgive them father, for they know not what they do.
You don't say.

In my dream, I tread waters with blue sharks,
recognize and respect our boundaries.
I am private like a cat and cover prodigious territories.

Contrary to the bargain struck, I leave unscathed
while you scrape for body bags and coffins
among black adders on the battlefields

of a bankrupt and barbaric country.
Give me spikenard, bergamot and cardamom
to soothe my aches, regulate beta particles,

cardio rhythm, and I'll bounce back.
I'll conjugate myself for you, punctuate every chord,
breathe through the dread, contrive convictions,

pucker my lips to cradle teeth and mouth.
It's cataclysmic, I'm cracked
open, bewildered and brazen.

Die ganze Nacht, folge ich dir.
I drink from the strange architecture of the cup offered.
Wir sind verrückt, aber du weiß es nicht.

When the knife feels like silk against the skin,
you can't tell the blade.
And when you lose your balance, you're over the edge,

the blood is spilled,
you're soaked in it
with no one to clean up the mess.

Stagger through darkness.
Träume ich?
I don't distinguish the dream from the physical.

Hélène Cardona

The Roman Empire

The lady in the park ducks her head when passing me
and veers a little to one side to keep from touching me.

I understand. She only wants to get out of the park alive
with her aging, high-strung Boston terrier,

and I retract my flesh as much as possible
to let her by. We know,

Each time a man and woman pass, each
time a man and woman pass each

time a man and woman pass
each other on an empty street,

it is an anniversary—
as if history was a cake made from layer after layer
of women's bodies, decorated with the purple, battered

faces of dead girls.
A visitor from outer space, observing us

from some hidden vantage place
would guess at some terrible historical event

of which our politeness is the evidence-
the man, attempting to look harmless;

the woman trying not to seem afraid.
Look at that dogwood tree flowering nearby, with a bird in it.

After you. No, after you.

Tony Hoagland

Manifesto

Watch my sister-in-law, vegan,
snap the leg off a roasted chicken
and you'll get it: how easily
the body is unmade. It's the carving plate,
to dinner, a hungry family set to feast
on thigh, breast, and wing
of decapitated creature.
Whose mind, the philosopher asked,
is inconsequential in its absence?
Not my sister-in-law's, stalked
by thoughts of home invasion:
late at night, alone, in bed half-dreaming
when she wakes to a window shattered,
footfall nearing her room
where she squints into outer darkness
and sees nothing but her own fear,
till he's on her: growling
hot into her ear, his stench
all sweat and sperm and beer,
pinning her at knife-point to her sheet—
how horrifying the eaters' smiles
at the plate of skinned meat, broken bones.

Seth Michelson

Hell on Earth
1992-95

Vilina Vlas, rape camp, shame.
Girls forced on concrete damp, shame.

Father top of daughter, knife
to his neck, stares at lamp, shame.

Amale, a child so young, twelve
times one night. Labeled *kurva,* shame.

Beaten by day, nighttime we wait.
Once more the brute, raw cramps, shame.

A name, an age but not by law.
Rape baby, no record stamped, shame.

Alice-Catherine Jennings

Notes:

Vilina Vlas was a main detention facility for Bosniak prisoners during the Bosnian War. It is estimated that 200 women and young girls were systematically raped and beaten by the Serbs at *Vilina Vlas.* After the war, Vilina Vlas was reopened as a hotel and medical rehabilitation center.

Kurva is the word for whore in Serbian.

For Shame

It's a veil that burns
the crown of your head,
spills down your face,
shoulders, breasts, belly,
your private parts,
leaving its telltale
stain at your feet.

The veil is transparent.
You must stand there naked.
They're all there, of course,
chanting the familiar chorus:
you were always   why didn't you
you are still   you shouldn't
you will never be ...

You want the earth
to turn into a deep
lake you can sink into,
but you must listen,
for your eyes are theirs,
they see only you,
homely cousin
of vain Narcissus,
the one who stuttered,
faltered and fell,
the one with no defenses,
who is indefensible,
the one it is easy to keep quiet.

You watch them stir the water.
So much silt, so many clouds.
Poor orphan, poor dear,
if only you could see yourself.

Debra Kaufman

Shed

In the wood shed
I found my uncle's magazines.

Snooping out of boredom,
looking for a wrench
to loosen a question in my body,

I flipped along glossy women
in kitchens without sinks
and refrigerators without food,
where bored housewives released
frustrations by
fucking the plumber,

where gardeners were pulled into pool houses
by college freshmen, their pig tails
doing most of the raking;
I saw women and horses
and women and circles of men
and women and women.

There seemed to be no shortage of women.

Being eleven with the drain pulled
on my wondered lust, my eyes
began to see sex everywhere,

in the plunging of stopped toilets,
in gas tanks being filled, in the pool halls
where my father circled his cue.

How the world moaned and pumped,
and hope flashed fluorescently through the blinds.

I lost my virginity three years later
to a girl without a name,
a neighbor in my curiosity about the body.

Before we did it, she said,
I don't make sounds during sex
and she didn't, just waited blankly,
waited to have emotion scribbled on her.

Eventually, love marked me
with a woman who walked with tumultuous hips—
she made bathrooms and classrooms more exciting,

and proved old Walt right— the body does
electric— when a kiss jumps the body—

as love is the leap of moment suspended
between jumping and landing, learning
and knowing, quitting and starting again

and it hurts more than just in skin
to walk because your walked away from,
and no hurt scatters, no love vanishes,
and no sorrow dissipates or forgives,
and no words can be eaten.
Nothing can be eaten.

And her climbing up a balcony on the second
floor to break in through the sliding glass door
to leave, on a puffed pillow, music she made for you

wont screw back together what was shed.
No one wants to leave the comfort of wood,
or finally say goodnight. I wish the world
had left me cuddled with boxes and magazines,

with boxed wine and videos of Vegas.
Can another cigarette break keep
the shell of sleep from cracking,

stay the flashes of her bent under another man?
Wondering if she is across the country, or the street,
how can I stop her monuments, not hear her again?

David Tomas Martinez

The Detective Asks Me What He Said

He'd pinch the breath
from my lungs
with two fingers
if I tried to scream.
That's what he said.
Said he'd been laid
more times than he
could count but had never
surprised a woman
in her sleep before.
I was his first.
He said that.
Said my body would be
more ready that way.
Said I should be honored
I was chosen
out of all the fillies
in first floor apartments
with their windows lifted
to let out the heat.
As if I should be patient
since he was a virgin of sorts
and it was up to me
to make this the experience
he had always wanted.
As if I ought to understand
I'd be the one to whom
he'd measure all the rest
which was a big responsibility
if I stopped to think about it.
He said that.

Shoshauna Shy

'Look at That Bitch Go!'[1]

I'd   [hit bone finish smash
      bang do slay pop
      nail pound take out tap
      ram drill screw]   that

B. T. Shaw

---

[1]Transcript, Baghdad air strike; July 27, 2007.

Verge

The boy who is about to rape me
Is skinny, small.
Much younger, too;
Only a sophomore.

The way he cuts up in French class
Has charmed me.
His accent is terrible,
And he never conjugates his verbs,
Even now, after three semesters.

I play him a song on my stereo
While the party whirls on
Outside my bedroom door.
I'm wondering only if
A senior should admit to liking
A boy so young.

When this song is over,
And the next one begins,
He will pin me down on my own bed,
Hold my arms
Against the mattress with his left hand,
And rip my jeans off with his right.
He will penetrate me,
And then he will say,

Wiggle.

And in the end,
Hushed as the snow falling outside
My locked window,
Silent as the icy rings
On a far-away planet,
I will do it,
Too ashamed to call out
From beneath him.

But that moment hasn't come yet.

Bono still hums on the Panasonic.
Elyse and Ashley giggle in the next room.
Trey bumps drunkenly into a hallway wall
And laughs. Ha ha. Ha ha.
The faintest aroma of pot
Wafts in from under the door, and
The semi-darkness of my bedroom
Swirls with anticipation.

I tuck my hair behind my ear,
Stare down at my bare feet.
The boy inches closer,
Fingering a stapler on my desk.
I say a quick prayer to my Creator:
Thank you. Thank you. Thank you for
Sending my parents out of town.

I'm swaying just a little,
As the song fades out
And he moves toward me.
I'm thinking, God, here it comes. . . .

Should I let a sophomore kiss me?
Does he really, really like me?
Would he—maybe—be bold enough
To ask me to my prom
In the Spring?

                                        Leila Allen

Some Girls

The Rape-aXe is a latex sheath embedded with shafts of sharp, inward-facing barbs that would be worn by a woman in her vagina.
— Wikipedia

1. *some girls rape easy.*
-state representative roger rivard

2. *i wish i had teeth down there.*
-rape survivor in south africa

somesomesome
some easy girls
rape easy some
girls girls girls
easy. so.me easy.
me easy. me the girl
in your mouth. some.
which ones representative?
the ones who beckon men
like fire ants with sweet pink
peony breath. curse this
flesh, too much entrance,
not enough weapon. easy
rape. another name for
death. no grave but
my whole body. no
roses. no balloons. no
memorial site to mark
the end of her. you
will never know how
sick the descent, how
the girl in the mirror isn't
you anymore, not girl any
more more more
easy woman, thighs
spread and yellowed
as treasure map, chest
closed tight as clam
over pearl, ghost of the
girl. girl died in your
mouth. in your bed.
nothing easy.
nothing easy.
all hard.
ghostgirl.
womannow.
somenobody.

wishwishwish
teeth i had
down down down
there i had. i. i. i.
downthereteeth.
venus flytrap elephant
ivory sharpened
vaginadaggers
ready, glistening
nightflower.
killerstarfish.
it will not be me in
the hospital this time:
no more rape test kits.
rape trap removal kits.
emergency room
overflowing with impaled
men screaming, clutching
themselves. now you
know how sick. i
dreamed this. woke
smiling, blood dripping
from my lips, its that
time of the month. moon
make madwoman of me.
men so scared of our red
but so quick to pull it out
of us like ribbon from
magician's throat.
i'd prefer to love you
but i'll kill you if i must.
before i let you dig
another grave in me.
bless this flesh, the
way it beckons, bless
the trap. the blood.
the truth is in the teeth.

Molly Pershin Raynor

The Girl in the Room

she was the girl who could be
squeezed between two boys, plied
with jokes, compliments, their minnow fingers
sampling her breasts accidentally as they passed
liquor across her; when she tried to pause, hold them
off, they told her how fun she was, how beautiful,
and tipped the bottle up to her mouth, pouring
in the musk of ocean, bleach of the sheets,
cajoling her into one more, don't worry,
they had time before they had to go down
to the beach for the others.

And when she stumbled they held her up,
helped her take another drink for good luck.
And when she collapsed they stretched her
down atop the bed stripped off her blouse and skirt,
held aside her covering arms, so they could pour
a final shot, until her legs failed to cross
and their hands pulled at her like fish tearing bait.

They took smiling selfies with their prize,
the one boy slamming, the other yanking
her hair back to jam her mouth.
Done, they waved the others up
from the pool to rake and flip, frenzy
on the girl in the room,

                              who only

came along because she wanted to
have friends, so grateful to be asked.

And when she awoke on the floor,
to the memory of blurred gargoyle faces,
her skin reeking of semen and whiskey,
head pounding, bruises riddling her lips
and thighs, she stumbled
to her room; the other girls rolled their eyes
and sneered 'Unh huh' to her cry
she'd been raped; she was the one, the slut
they weren't, the whore trying to ruin couples
by blaming the boys she chose to fuck;

she was the girl in the room,
a daughter, a mother, a wife,
the woman I love,
the woman who loves
despite.

Richard Krawiec

Dormitory

Palms to knees, I steady myself — drunk, and swaying between the
two, who pass a bottle through me, each to each. The math means
I have two drinks for every one of theirs, and they coax-cajole, taunt
me into continuing, and when I slow, tip the liquid for me, until the
room begins to dip and tilt on an unseen axis, with me at its center.
You are the sun, they whisper, but it seems impossible that the sun
feels dizzy like this. I am trying to form words I don't remember
how to say, something like *No* something like *I need to go* but my
mouth is thick and slow. I try to rise but they catch my sleeve, assure
me, lie, tell me friends are on their way back to us. My legs aren't
listening anyway, and I have lost track of where I am. I groan, push
the bottle away, which seems to be a cue — they lay me back on the
bed. The mattress is soft against my shoulders, soft, all I want to
do is sink into it, all I want to be is released, to not be here, in the
center of this. I will give anything if they will let me sleep. I feel
fingers move on me as from far away, on my hips, on my thighs, faint
as echo. One is on top of me as my eyes are closing, folding me into
sleep. Sleep, with dreams of oceans tossing my body.

Melissa Hassard

Rape Culture

Mike brings back punch
to this girl he just met as she
spins in the contingent
beauty of voices around her.
The drink sings in her
mind its tales of beautiful
submission and she smiles
and says *you know I like
feminism all right but what's the
point. — That's it exactly,* he says.
What year is it in this world
where we don't need to be
equal? What's the weather like
where they are? When the rain
falls they leave the party
and walk toward their dorm.
It's weird how his dick
already feels thrust into
the idea of her, her cold wet
hands, the way she keeps
pockets of warmth within
her coat that his hands crawl
their way inside.

In this world where they think
they're already equal,
he does not remove his jacket
for her until they are back
at his place, the water dripping
through the ceiling, her mouth
hanging slack like something
he wants to tear open.

Mike, ask yourself what
you really want to tear
open: is it yourself
or some idea of love
that always involves breaking?
Ask yourself: if you do
what you are thinking
and you wake and knives

of sunlight tear you
into the day and she lies
unmoving next to you, broken,
ask yourself how you could ever
tear her up without eviscerating
something in yourself? Ask yourself:
why can you not wear her
black stilettos and exoskeletal
blue dress and be spun
in the deep voices of men
like spidersilk until you glisten
with the intent to be consumed?

                                        Kenan Ince

The Day I Saw My Rapist at the Corner Texaco

Part 1

I remember holding the fuel nozzle in my hand,
staring at him for what seemed an eternity.

I was bisected –
    half of me desperate
    to spray gasoline across the concrete divide
    and light a match,

while the other half
    wanted to peel away my skin
    to swap with another human to hide.

My babies –
    all three of them lined up in their car seats
    in the backseat of my Honda.

Two little girls peacefully asleep,
while their brother pointed his chubby finger
    at a ladybug on the windshield
    and laughed.

Part 2: 16 Years Later

I knew this day would come.
The day I would have to let my secret out,
tell my story.
For ignorance is dangerous,
not bliss.

I have to make the hard choice –
remove my children's veil of invincibility.
Make them understand,
rape isn't something that only happens
to *other* people.

Their heads bow down like wilting roses.
They reach for my trembling hand.
We hold each other. We cry.
I can feel my shame
morphing into courage.

I didn't teach my daughters
how to *avoid* rape that day.
I didn't buy them a whistle.
Instead, I taught my son
the horrid ugliness of the crime
against a woman, a girl, a mother, a sister…

…and when I told their father about our talk,
he asked me if I told them
what I was wearing.

Shawn Aveningo

Assaulted
(a one-act play)

(In 2011 & 2012 in Brooklyn, women were sexually assaulted as they exited the R train station between Park Slope & Sunset Park stops. Police sent out a notice that women should avoid wearing skirts until the assailant was caught. In Manhattan an elderly woman was raped in Central Park during the day. Officers later claimed they never told women what not to wear; they simply pointed out patterns and advised women to heed those warnings.)

Officer: You were wearing a skirt, is that right?

Woman: Yes, but-

Officer: Ok, so you were wearing a skirt, you admit that

Woman: Yes, but

Officer: Please don't interrupt. The facts are very important in rape cases. Understood?

Woman: Yes, it's just that

Officer: Ok, so you were wearing a skirt and what time was the erm incident, did you say?

Woman: About 1:30

Officer: AM or PM?

Woman: AM

Officer: So, you were out at 1:30 in the morning, wearing a skirt and, well, let me ask you, what did you expect to happen

Woman: I'm sorry?

Officer: Yes, well, you should be sorry, because well, it's like you, you know, I mean, it's like you brought this on yourself

Woman: What? I was

Officer: Yeah, yeah, minding my own business, etcetera etcetera. The fact remains, you were out at a godforsaken hour, alone, wearing a skirt, what did you expect?

Woman: I. . .I want to press charges

Officer: Ma'am, you can press charges, but like I said, a woman walking alone at 1:30 in the morning wearing a skirt, in this city, I don't know what you expected

Woman: I expect the police to understand that the only person to blame for rape is the rapist.

Officer:

Woman: Now, I'd like to press charges, please

Metta Sáma

The Long Silence

1

She took every pill
of a cramps prescription,
slipping down the dark well

of her bed. When they found her
she couldn't be roused,
the blood so bad

the medics thought
she had aborted herself.
Entered again

by doctors, needles, machines,
stripped, strapped down,
unable to answer

the clipboard questions
when   how
voluntary or involuntary

just to make it all
go away
voluntary   she lied.

2

She had seen the remaining light
from an Indian summer evening
receding through curtains

he had not even bother to close,
heard the click of the red wink
of his clock notching time

the voices outside, passing,
saying it sure sounded like
someone was having a good time.

No one heard *help me*
as he held her hobbled body
hard to the floor

forcing her,
his last whole sentence to her
don't tell me you didn't enjoy it.

3

She never told anyone,
and shrunk from her brother's brag
of girls who'd do anything for him.

Even he, the one, finding her late
on a walkway at night, leered,
you're not still hung up

on that are you?
Twenty years from now
you'll feel different.

Twenty years,
twenty years
of watching that sunlight

die on the other side
of the glass, a night
of brute witness coming in.

In her mind, she prays,
It is not death
I wish for you

it is a daughter.

Deborah Pope

Sunday Afternoon Stroll
Richmond Town, Bangalore

We slip on shards
pavement heaped with broken bricks,
                    garbage, a sleeping dog.
Men loiter outside the corner chai shop,
stop their chatter to stare at us,
chat again, then stare some more.
We step off the sidewalk to pass by them,
narrowly miss being hit by a ball
thrown by neighborhood boys
playing cricket in the center of the road.

Where are the girls?
my six year old daughter wonders aloud.
She looks around at the apartments
                    surrounding us—
for young girls and their mothers
who might be looking at us
through narrow window slits cut out
                    of blank faced walls.

Ahead, I avert my daughter's eyes
                    just in time
as we pass a vagrant,
hands dug deep inside his pant pockets,
waving to us with his penis.

Athena Kashyap

43

Two Sisters

Two sisters walking. One
was molested by their father.
You wonder which is which,
if the one walking faster

spends her life fleeing a house on fire
only she can sense, if the one
with arms crossed over her chest
as if winter lived on in her body?

The shorter hem, or would it be the longer,
trying too late to hide? If the one
with no children or the one with four.
The one who startles when approached

from behind, or the one who laughs
with a hand pressed to her mouth,
afraid the ash will escape.
Both stiffen for the embrace.

Both stare at the shadow behind a man.
Is it the prettier one or the less talkative?
Asking these questions makes you realize
you must think like their father.

You must go back in time and decide
which child is more precious
and what precious means.
You must decide, when forming

the glass shards into laurels,
which child you may crown
without bloodying
your own hands.

Karen Skolfield

Against Forgetting the 276

Elizabeth Joseph played hide-and-seek.

One afternoon you open the door
to your younger sister's bedroom,
and her absence becomes
two things: A school uniform. A notebook.
For how many hours you will sit,
banging your head against the wall,
trying to understand what thoughts
bloomed in her brain
when she scribbled down those notes
about the solar system,
on the pages you cradle in your hand:
Stop acting so small.
You are the universe in ecstatic motion.

Monica Enoch liked to sing.

And what shrines you will create
for that school uniform:
where best to put it –
the first two weeks, in her room, like a homing device,
anxiously awaiting her return;
later, in the window, hanging in plain sight,
in case, wherever she is, she has forgotten what
Home looks like;
or after a month, sliced into little strips of fabric,
which you carry in your pockets
and let fall wherever you go,
each one fluttering to the pavement
like a trail of dying dreams behind you,
because Bring Back Our Girls
is not bringing back your girl.

Rhoda Peters' favorite food was rice and beans.

You begin to realize that
your mother will never stop
cooking your sister's favorite food
every night for dinner,
and your father will stop
saying Too Much Salt
because he knows
this is not the taste of carelessness,

it is the taste of tears – and you,
you are so swollen with pain that
you will sidestep the pink
polka-dotted barrettes she left
hurriedly on the bathroom floor
that morning months ago,
as if by touching them,
you will shatter.

She is not a number,
this Nigerian girl;
she was the remote control
of your family's life,
and now your world
has become static.

Vishnupriya Krishnan

Excavation at Kampsville

You clutched *Archeology* magazine
in your twelve-year old hand,
dreamed of mortars and pestles,
flint knapping, perfect arrow points
as we drove to the banks of the Illinois River.

Archeology is a destructive science,
the field director announced
then told of an amateur intruder
who dug a nine-foot shaft
into the Maples Russell Burial Mound,
concealed his path with a grassy man-hole cover,
sneaked breaths through a long rubber hose,
and, by lantern, raped the tomb
of all its wonders, even the tiny
bird heads carved from the teeth of bears.

Each morning for a week, we arose at five,
eased by raft across the sleeping river
to the natural levee, descended
into our designated squares.
Each day we troweled deeper into our pit
until our shovels grazed the midden
of the vanished Woodland people.
Then we scraped the earthen membrane,
combed debris across a sifting screen,
immersed our hands in the rubble,
groped for pebbles big enough
to percolate in the lab.

But none of us once wrapped fingers
around the handle of an adze, stroked
the flake scar of a projectile point,
or cradled a single pottery shard.
Only once, a girl shouted from a nearby square
and we scrambled to crowd
and gape at the week's big find:
a swirling hint of brown,
a bare streak of red.
A clam bake perhaps, the director shrugged.

Now, six years later, you hand me
a secret buried too deep back then
for even you to unearth:
When you were as young and fresh
as the beanfields along the Illinois levee,
a slackjawed invader probed
your hidden crevices with cravings
sharp as flint, smashed tiny treasures
with blunt fingers, dug deep
shafts into your still soft folds.

My mind freezes. No words of comfort come.
I can only think to send you back to that humid
July in Kampsville. You must go back,
plot the coordinates of your shame,
descend into the muggy pit, tunnel
to your damp secret passage, finger
the tender mound of skin below,
sift through the filth and fragments
until you find precious in the center
of your net, in the palm of your hand,
the hard gem of you.

Janice Moore Fuller

Light Switch

He switches on the light.
I do not want it on.
My eyes too small for spectacles,
he still calls them that,
turn to the shelves,
full of Whimsies and stiff Spanish dolls.
He folds his trousers neatly,
the belt coiled on top.
He likes to switch the light on,
I step into my dark,
and fill it with light waves of music notes,
and singing monkeys in fat green trees,
streams of lemonade and a small blue boat,
with stars that smile at the moon,
and mermaids that want to play.
And very carefully,
I place a small blue house
in a large poppy field,
make red checked curtains
and a door I can lock.

Lizzie Holden

If the Girl is a Horror Movie Starlet

Slice by slice, curls of rosewood peel
away. The girl poses on the floor,
nude, the father re-creating his daughter.
She'll never leave him, this wood girl.
He holds a chisel, she,
palms empty, arms modestly
crossed against the cold. Her legs
bent, thighs, for once, pressed
together, the girl, the father, watching
the sculpture form shoulders
and elbows, a rose vein in the wood
emerging from the neck, trailing
between breasts and thighs
as if filled with blood. Or,

thin as a daddy long legs sliding
down the roof of the girl's green
Volkswagen bug, the car only in second
gear, driving slowly, as if the girl
is still miles away from the crash. His thinner-
than-a-pin legs track the windshield,
the girl afraid to crank open the window.
She switches on wipers – dismembered
legs, his smashed body, smear
the glass. The wipers continue
to scrape back and forth,
until the credits roll. Now the father

sits strapped in a lounge
chair. Otherwise, his demented
brain would let him sneak away: his genius.
The girl sits beside him dipping a spoon
into a bowl of chocolate ice cream.
She slides it into his mouth.
Greedily he swallows, nods
his head, unable to speak,
but asking for more.

Sue William Silverman

Tongue and Groove

The tongue and groove is nailed to silence.
A fire took it to the ground and would not
let the boards speak in tongues of that old house
built by grease under Granddaddy's nails.
Grandma graded tobacco in the back room
in summer, quilted in winter. When a marriage
ran its course they all moved home,
ten to twelve in the three-room shotgun shack.
The walls did not murmur of Clyde's lust
for young girls. God crippled him up, sent
him to the back room where his scoundrel eyes
could not hurt little girls. How many daughters
kept beatings inside until a bruise shone
through a worn blouse? Grandma brought them
home to the safety of walls painted a new coat
of bright blue every spring. She never faltered
when it came to keeping secrets, watched in
silence her mother wither away in the iron
hospital bed. The weight of these stories
blistered the enamel, warped the tongue and groove.

Marty Silverthorne

The Huntsman

> "Whatever may be their use in civilised societies,
> mirrors are essential to all violent and heroic action."
> — Virginia Woolf

I was only seven when he touched me
So I headed for the hills

Where I found the littlemen, sexless,
Which suited me just fine

But a mirror of my own forewarned
He'll come for you one day

So I wished the laces tighter
The comb sharper

Welcomed the apple
With anxious, blood-red mouth

(It was not about Mother;
I had never known a woman to be kind)

Sivan Butler-Rotholz

Adjourned

*In 2014, a 29-year-old Georgia mother pleaded guilty to crimes
that included rape and aggravated child molestation.*

Long before the judge called you "the vilest bitch I've ever met,"
before the details shook the courtroom to tears,
before the bailiff had to get up and walk out,
before 30 years in prison and lifetime probation as a sex offender,
before your Macon home, before Crawford County, before the
        abandoned trailer,

                before you held your daughter down
                so your boyfriend could have his way,
            before it became an "every night thing,"
              long before your girls were 6 and 8,

    someone told you, "This is how men show you they love you."
             and you believed it.

Kathleen Nalley

Gretel Writes to Her Mother

Other girls' mothers
would have eaten
dirt
      fire
any man's dick
rather than leave their children
alone with a shithole drunk for a father
in a country that spits out women
like sand from a desert faucet.
And they do.

Other girls' mothers
offer themselves
to soldiers, mercenaries, thugs,
mark door posts and mattresses
with their own blood and vain hopes
before watching their daughters
disappear,
    nameless

to all but their mothers,
who cry themselves to sleep
still calling their names.

Addy Robinson McCulloch

Frame

This year is burning
   from the inside out;
      blossom
         under the apples.

From the inside out
  add that fire—
    under the apples,
      just bitten.

     Add that fire.
In the inner corners,
just bitten,
beg for beauty.

     In the inner corners,
  blossom,
beg for beauty—
this year
     is burning.

E. Kristin Anderson

This is a found poem. Source material: "Be the New Hot Girl @ School" by Amanda Elser. *Seventeen,* August 2014, pages 62-68.

Astray

When my father says he has no idea
why I've parted ways with my mother—
what is so devastating that I can't forgive—I tell him again

that she's befriended the man who groomed me for sex
when I was 12; that she forgave him for whatever
I'd imagined he'd done.

Well I don't need to hear, he interrupts, *anything about that...*
then steers us toward the damage we do to ourselves—
Our-Selves, he emphasizes so I understand—

when we let fear rule. He poses questions for me to consider:
Is fear in charge? Am I an adult, for crying out loud, or a little girl?
Do I think Dr. King let fear stop him? that Earhart threw up her hands

because *Oh my goodness, that's just too far to fly! Who was that guy who said
'Let no man fear anything but fear itself'? Lemme tell you something:
You know who had stage fright but got up in front of people anyhow?
You wanna know?*

Marlon Brando. Absolutely terrified.

Stephanie Levin

Belts

No, I won't
stand still
while she
whips me
with Daddy's
belt. She's mad
because I won't
clean my room
and said, "I hate
you, you ugly
old witch."
It's Saturday.
I want to watch
Mighty Mouse
and eat a frozen
Twinkie.
I run from room
to room as she
lashes at my legs,
leaping as if
we're playing
hop-scotch
without chalk
or rocks. When
he comes home,
I point at red
welts on
my legs. "See
what she did to
me." He
says, "You
deserved it."

He unbuckles
his belt, unzips
his jeans. I'm
drunk. I don't
want him to,
he's blonde with black
moles on his back
like dead flies.
It's Saturday
night, our first
date. I don't
move, I don't
say "No!"
or "Stop!"
He's on top
pushing
inside until
I break
in two: one
girl stays
on the bed
while the other
one floats
to the ceiling
to watch.
Whatever
you do,
you're
gonna get
what's
coming
to you.

Beth Copeland

Flower Girl Dress

"Girls fall like stones in our family," my father says. "Too many for bridesmaids." Rosita, the bride, says, "Maria, you must be the flower girl because you are the smallest and were the last to fall. It is O.K. to be thirteen and a flower girl. In God's eyes, your innocence makes you younger."

The organ's wedding march shakes the saints in their niches. Their plastered faces drop flakes of paint like pieces of puzzled grace. I follow my sisters down the aisle. Their shoulders shift in blue dresses like awakened wings. Clouds from the desert bump the windows like ancestors who have forgotten doors. The lace in my white dress sings against its satin slip as I toss red rose petals into the air. They hover, catch in the haze of incense, then float gently to the floor.

This is where I place my mind, when the men pound into me, claw my small breasts with chicken-feet hands, and finish with goat-like cries. They are so dirty, sweaty. Their bodies smell of farms, truck grease, fumes of poisoned fields. I wipe up with paper towels, shower twenty-five times a day. I am never clean.

For good luck and many boy children, relatives rain rice over the couple. Birds gather in trees, sharpen beaks against twigs, while armadillos settle their accordion shells under bushes to await the feast.

Today, I would lick the rice from the street, devour the stale piece of cake I tucked under my pillow to dream the face of my future husband, a kind man. I would dig the nectar from the slender throats of the lilies in my sister's bouquet, eat the sweet petals to their bare stems.

The pimps starve me. The men who pay like me skinny, child-like as their daughters. Is this what they would do to their girls, if they could? If the daughters knew, would they sit so comfortably in their fathers' laps letting them unbind their braids?

"You'll rot in this bed," the pimps say. "If you try to escape, we'll kill Rosita. Bring you her finger, ringed in gold." At night, when the men stop coming, I unroll the paper towels, cover the bed so their smells won't rise and soil my dreams.

I start down the church aisle again. My lace dress swishes against its satin slip. My sisters' wings turn into fins as they float away in a blue river. I call out. Only the ghosts framed in the windows answer, gasping into the organ pipes. I toss handfuls of red petals into the air. Fistfuls rise into the smoke, harden into the morning vows of stones. They beat my body into the day that is.

Carolyn Dahl

First Marriage

After the wedding his fist flew, connected.
My face was bruised. It caught us by surprise,
that " sudden blow," as in the Yeats sonnet
I had to write a paper on for class.

My eye was bruising. We were both surprised.
He'd never touched me that way before.
I still had to write the paper for my class.
He hit me like his father hit his mother.

He'd never touched me that way before,
but he'd seen it as a boy. I couldn't concentrate.
He hit me like his father used to hit his mother,
and we were that old pattern, pitiful and trite.

He'd seen it as a boy. How could I concentrate
on Yeats's question, far away as a Grecian vase?
My husband had become his father, another wife-beater.
He cried and brought me ice for my face.

That question—circular as a Grecian vase—
soothes like music, like a healing balm.
My young husband cried, brought me ice for my face.
I stopped crying before he did. You have to stay calm.

It soothed like music, healing like a balm,
and I covered my bruises with make-up.
I stopped crying. You have to stay calm.
I studied the poem—"Being so caught up…"

I put on my Cover Girl concealer too thick—
while Leda "put on his knowledge with his power."
I wrote the paper. I had to get caught up
with the class. My professor asked, *Is something the matter?*

Here's what you can learn from a man's powerful
fist: Pretend you're okay. Say it's no big thing.
Guilt just riles them up again. Smile, say it doesn't matter.
Yeats's sonnet made "being mastered" sound thrilling.

I'll bet Leda didn't say a thing,
lying in that "white rush" until he was finished
and dropped her. Yeats made rape sound thrilling.
Everything connects. That swan, his fist.

LaWanda Walters

A Leveling

He brought us here, to this juniper desert,
across Midwestern state borders into broken promise,

sloughing family fragments like tire treads along the way.
I-80 rose up like Hell's Backbone, egoistic and narrow-

sighted with drops on either side of slight rails.
We should have been safe in the valleys,

miles away from Boulder Mountain . . .
And yet I learned to fear altitudes,

the uncertainty of my own feet,
the distant perspective of abandonment.

Two years gone. Maybe it wasn't long enough.
The knee-locking dread never subsides.

Instead, vertigo sets in on each downward step,
handrails clenched each time I try high heels

and the teetering always sets me down bare.
How can I be bowed into such spinelessness,

faint at the sight of red clay cliffs and sloping pines—
a grand staircase. Father Escalante would pray for me

to forgive. He would level my landings. He would lead
me to grace.

Trish Hopkinson

Soup

When his knuckles graze my cheek,
the blow lands soft, almost gentle,
as if he's decided in midair
to take it back, but somehow can't.
Most people keep eating; one couple
eyes us from the corner banquette.
An unvoiced *o* sticks in my throat,
suspended, as if trapped in amber.
Legs, wings viscid with resin,
cluster of eyes filming, fixing,
extinguishing: I pretend – like
the waiter – that nothing's happening.

Katherine E. Young

Grip

Held at gunpoint in your custom
Econoline, the road hemmed in blackberries,
scrub willow, salt breeze and skunk
cabbage somewhere along the Oregon
coast, and the barrel pressing hard
against my temple, I knew by your thin
voice and trembling hand, that your knuckles
were white on the rubber grip.

Carmel Mawle

Blackberries

Crawling through cool tunnels between the canes, grass soaking
through your jeans, dodging thorns and hunting berries in their
fat clusters, hanging thick as grapes, but softer, so soft they dissolve
on fingertips, they have to be taken, sweet and bleeding, on the
tongue, like a lover whose own skin was broken once, or more than
once, who can never forget that pain, it comes back sometimes,
shuddering strong, something like pleasure the memory that rips
the covers off who you are now and lays you raw before the person
you want to have and the person you want to be, sobbing fear you
try to bury and wish would go away but it never does, you can only
hope to shield your lover from the spines and offer up the tart black
fruit of who it made you, hope the harvest is worth the work and
all those ragged scars.

Sonja Johanson

Gleaner

A wooden ladder leans against his peach tree,
uprights touching a laden branch. When his fist

thrusts out at me, I'm quicker to cover my face.
Light sparks between my folded arms like light

flaming through a bushel basket, pure shimmer
but broken. I'm learning to live in this orchard.

I crouch to pick through the windfall peaches,
choosing the least punctured, the least bruised.

Penelope Scambly Schott

The Gun

What does a gun mean
to a woman-child?
A small Italian make
that fits in the palm of her hand
like a cold, smooth stone
and rests so quietly
beneath her pillow.

What does a gun mean
to a "good little girl"
who always tries to please,
condemned to drown a little daily?
Who waits in the night
full of emptiness,
suspended between love and suspicion,
to hear the sound
of a key in the lock.

What does a gun mean
when she walks barefoot
on the alien sandy road,
the air full of hopelessness,
ten miles from nowhere,
a small child clinging to each hand,
transportation locked and forbidden
to her for days at a time?

What does a gun mean
when only long sleeves
can hide the bruises
that bloom on her flesh
where the fists of the man
who gave her the gun for protection
left his marks of ownership?

Rebecca Pierre

Transcript of Court Hearing for a Restraining Order

Judge:	"Mrs. B, is this your complaint?"
Ex-wife:	"Yes, your Honor."
Judge:	"Is Mr. B. here?"
Ex-husband:	"Right here"
Judge:	"Good, then we can begin. Do you understand what a restraining order does? It directs you to stay away from her and leave her alone."
Ex-husband:	"Well…"
Judge:	"What's that you said?"
Ex-husband:	"I said no white man is going to tell me what to do."
Judge:	"Mr. B., I hear your opinion of these proceedings, but it is beside the point. This hearing is to address your ex-wife's complaints. This is a courtroom and what we say here has the force of law. We work to end domestic abuse.
Ex-husband:	"I don't care what happens to her anymore. I lost all sexual desire for her when she called the police.
Judge:	"Mr. B., if you continue to disrupt, you risk being charged with contempt of court. Is that what you want, a week in jail?
Ex-husband:	"No, your Honor,"
Judge:	"Fine, we can move on then. The interlocutory judgment of divorce was dated March 1965, six months ago, correct?
Ex- wife:	"Yes."
Judge:	"And you're asking to leave the city?"
Ex-wife:	"Yes, your Honor, in the East Bay I'll be near my father."
Judge:	"Good, send your new address to the Alameda County D.A.'s Family Support division and they will contact our office here in the City, and will contact your ex. Is that clear, Mr. B?
Ex-husband:	"Yes, sir."
Judge:	"Should we discuss child visitation today or postpone?"
Ex-wife:	"I spoke to my sister-in-law about her watching them during his visits.
Ex-husband:	"No one tells me when I can see my children; I'd rather not see them at all until they're grown.

Cecile Lusby

Why I Stayed

The question isn't
why we fought
or why you put
your hands
around my neck
and broke me over
the purple plastic Ikea table
we used as a nightstand
next to the mattress
on the dank linoleum floor

but why I stayed with you
for many months more,
allowing myself to be strangled
from the inside out,
until I thought
there would be nothing left
for anyone else to hold.

Leslie Waugh

Why I Hate Silent Movies

I hate the heat because it reminds me
of the first time he slapped my face.
We were sitting on the sofa and he said
he did it because it was too hot outside.
Later he cried and kissed my feet,
said he would never. I hate flowers
because after he punched me
he got me ice and five bouquets: roses,
lilies, carnations, tulips, and daisies.
I hate jewelry because he bought me
a diamond necklace when he took me out
of the hospital, said *Love me love me love me.*
I hate silent movies because they resemble
my pain back then—all glare and no sound.
I hate bird cages because no matter
how many times I opened them,
those goddamn canaries wouldn't fly.
I hate nests because even years after I left
on that day when he strangled my birds,
my hands sometimes smell of feathers
and I still pull out straw pieces, twigs,
and his voice from my hair.

Zeina Hashem Beck

The Accident

I had no business there in the first place—
I'm putting on weight—but the counter help was all smiles,
Having survived the lunch hour crush. My husband and I
Ordered burgers and fries; I was in front, so I chose
A seat on the far side, back to the window.
I picked off two thin rings of onion; the fries were limp.
We were talking about some recent trouble,
Something about the car, maybe, both of us
Interested, me a little bitchy, so it was almost the way you turn
Instinctively, say from a spider web in a darkened hall,
How I looked across the restaurant and found her face,
Left cheekbone swollen to a baseball, the same eye blackened,
Heavy make-up, front tooth out in a jack-o-lantern grin
As she tried to look friendly to the young waitress
Her husband motioned over. He rested one hand
On his wife's shoulder, solicitous, the other waving
A lit cigarette, a small man, dark-haired, now laughing aloud,
Glancing at the uncombed head of his beaten wife again
Turning her back to the room, though not crowded,
All suddenly staring, reading the last few hours
Of those lives in a horror of recognition.
She cupped her hand shading the side of her face,
You could see lumps of vertebrae through her t-shirt,
And he kept on talking, smiling at her, with a slight tilt
Of his head, as if saying *poor baby, something happened to her,*
Good thing I'm here to take care of her, a car wreck,
A bad one, a smash-up, and all of us looked
And knew better. At the table with them was a little girl.
The man, the woman, the five-year-old daughter—
Even the man and the beaten woman had the same features,
As people do who have lived together for years. I couldn't see
The child's face. He was jotting a note on a small pad,
The waitress's name, as if to write a letter praising
Her fine service, and she smiled through her horror, she
Hardly more than sixteen, with clear pale skin. Next to us
A woman in permed hair and suit rose to leave, lunch untouched,
With her daughter. She carried a leather legal-size folder.
We left soon after, heads turned, not looking,
Because sometime the man and woman would go
Home to the privacy of a city apartment, no neighbors
Home all day to hear, but first I said, in the restaurant,

Across the room where he couldn't hear, *If I had a gun
I'd blow his brains out,* and I thought of that moment
Familiar from movies, the round black hole in the forehead
Opening, the back of the skull blowing out frame by frame
Like a baseball smashing a window, but no one near
Would've even been bloodied because no one was standing anywhere
Near him, his hand on the beaten woman's shoulder
Might as well have been yards from his body.

I was taught not to write about this. But my teacher,
A man with a reputation who hoped I would make
Good, never knew that I too have been hit in the face by a man.
He knew only my clumsy efforts to cast what happened
Into "characters," and he loved beauty in poetry.
Maybe what I had written was awkward. Maybe my teacher
Guessed what happened and forbade me writing it
For some good reason, he cared for me, or he feared
He too might've slapped my face, because I, like the character
In that first effort, was bitching to the heavens and a redneck
Boyfriend, and we argued outdoors, near a stack of light wood
Used to kindle the stove like everyone has
In the foothills of North Carolina. That day I railed
Like a caricature of a bitching redneck woman,
Hands on hips, sometimes a clenched fist, I was
Bitching, I think, as he planned some stupid thing
I hated, like fishing, pitching horseshoes, driving
To visit his mother on Sundays, her tiny house
Tangled in dirt roads where she sat in the kitchen dipping snuff.
Whatever he wanted to do was harmless,
But so was my shrieking, my furious pleading, an endless loop
Inside my head rolling *I want to be rid of him,* and he slapped me
Across my open mouth, I felt myself shut up and staggered,
Because he was a large man, and I was a large woman,
He had to make sure he hit me pretty hard,
Both of us strong and mad as hell, early
One Saturday morning, when he wanted to do what he wanted to do
And I wanted to keep him from it. He slapped me
Twice, open-handed, knocking me, open-handed, to my knees
In kindling, so my knees were scraped bloody and my hand
Closed on a foot and a half of inch-thick pine, and I stumbled up
Swinging, my eyes popping wide, till I brought it down
Hard across his shoulder, I saw how the rage on his face
Flashed to fear, just that quick, a second, or less,

And he turned to run but he made the wrong choice,
If he'd gone to the road I wouldn't've followed, but he ran
Inside my "duplex" apartment, an old country house
Cut in two. So I cornered him upstairs and knocked him out.
It was simple. He fell so hard, I thought, I've killed him;
I was throwing my clothes in a paper bag when I heard him
Sobbing. In the bathroom mirror I found the black eye and lop-sided lip,
And it seemed as if I might still take it back, the last ten minutes,
The chase, the beating, the high-pitched screaming,
The stubborn need to go fishing. But the make-up I disdained
In those years—I had just turned twenty—didn't do much
To cover the bruises. His face was clear. The knot on his head
Stopped swelling under ice. It was easy to tell him
To get the hell out and only regret it every other minute
Since there were no children, no marriage, even,
And I was young and believed I had proven
I was strong. I had beaten a man to his knees.
Months later I would go to college and stay safely there for years,
Not letting on to anyone the terrible thing I'd done, until I wrote
That clumsy poem with the unbelievable characters, and now I've tried
To do it again, this time with different characters, I've defied
My teacher, who meant for me to learn to write well,
Who meant for the world to think well of me,
And I am not sorry. If he asked why I would say
I had to do it, and that lie would be like the lie of living
Without telling, till one day seeing the beaten face,
What scared me most, the missing tooth, the tangled hair, the vertebrae,
The daughter. There is no use thinking what it means
About me to say this: I am not sorry. I might have killed
That man. I might have blown his brains out.

Lisa Lewis

Doctor's Office

You would not let me go alone. While you explained my clumsy
nature I memorized the symptoms of asthma. I studied the skin of
my hands. I read the front cover of *Green Eggs and Ham* at least
ten times. They instructed you to remain when I had my blood
drawn. Your eyes followed me as I left with her. Has he ever hurt
you? She frowned. Her pen lingered, poised over the clipboard.
I shook my head silently. She took the tears in my eyes for pain,
which they were, and I went the rest of the way with uneven steps,
the impression of your fist in my back.

Sharon Sitler

Triptych
for Caroline

I.

Texas firefighter kills girlfriend and then himself as she prepared to leave abusive relationship: report

BY NICOLE HENSLEY / NEW YORK DAILY NEWS/
Published: Friday, May 22, 2015, 4:06 PM/ Updated: Friday, May 22, 2015, 4:06 PM

Family of a Houston, Texas nurse knew something was wrong when she failed to pick up her young daughter from school.

Those fears were not unfounded — knowing she'd soon be leaving her abusive **firefighter** boyfriend — and led to the gruesome discovery of Caroline Minjares, 36, dead in **her** home. They also found her **boyfriend,** dead by taking his own life on Thursday night.

"She told me 'if **he** ever left her, **he** was going to kill her.' That's pretty much what ended up happening," Minjares' brother, Eduardo Minjares told KHOU-TV.

*A Houston **firefighter** is believed to have **killed his girlfriend,** Caroline Minjares, pictured, on **before taking his own life** at her home.*

It's believed Richard Deluna, **a** 40-year-old **firefighter** with Houston Fire Department, broke into Minjares' home as she slept after a nursing shift, **stabbed her to death** and then stuck around for several hours until the victim's mother called, authorities said.

He **claimed to be at work,** Deluna told the worried mother, but really, he **was** at Minjares' **home as she lay dead.** He then **killed himself,** authorities added.

Shortly after the phone call, Minjares' relatives burst into the home screaming 'where is she' before finding the bodies, neighbors told KPRC-TV.

"He's just a coward I don't know why he did this to our family," Eduardo Minjares added. "Our family is devastated."

Minjares and Deluna had been dating for about one year and had recently decided she would end their relationship, KHOU-TV reported.

A statement from Houston Professional Fire Fighters Association made no reference to the circumstances of Deluna's death, but said local firefighters were in mourning over the off-duty death.

"Our organization will strive to help support his brothers and sisters in the fire service, his family and his friends in this difficult time. Please keep his family and friends in your thoughts and prayers as answers are sought after this inexplicable tragedy," fire officials wrote to KPRC-TV.

Minjares, a nurse at Neighbors Emergency Center, leaves behind two daughters, ages 5 and 14.

II.

She was leaving.

leave (\lēv\) *verb:* to cause to remain as a trace or aftereffect, to fail to include or take along, to permit to be or remain subject to another's action or control.

She

was   *leaving*

                          him.

                          The cracked hinge,
                  the fractured pane

                  over the bedpost.

White-crowned sparrow on the barrel bolt latch, hollow-boned,

                  white-winged.

III.

Texas firefighter kills girlfriend and then himself as she prepared to leave abusive relationship: report

BY NICOLE HENSLEY / NEW YORK DAILY NEWS/
Published: Friday, May 22, 2015, 4:06 PM/ Updated: Friday, May 22, 2015, 4:06 PM

Family of a Houston, **Texas nurse knew something was wrong** when she failed to pick up her young daughter from school.

Those fears were not unfounded — knowing she'd soon be leaving her abusive firefighter boyfriend — and led to the gruesome discovery of Caroline Minjares, 36, dead in her home. They also found her boyfriend, dead by taking his own life on Thursday night.

"She told me 'if he ever left her, he was going to kill her.' That's pretty much what ended up happening," Minjares' brother, Eduardo Minjares told KHOU-TV.

A Houston firefighter is believed to have killed his girlfriend, Caroline Minjares, pictured, on before taking his own life at her home.

It's believed Richard Deluna, a 40-year-old firefighter with Houston Fire Department, broke into Minjares' home as **she** slept after a nursing shift, stabbed her to death and then stuck around for several hours until the victim's mother called, authorities said.

He claimed to be at work, Deluna told the worried mother, but really, he was at Minjares' home as **she** lay dead. He then killed himself, authorities added.

Shortly after the phone call, Minjares' relatives burst into the home screaming **'where is she'** before finding the bodies, neighbors told KPRC-TV.

"He's just a coward I don't know why he did this to our family," Eduardo Minjares added. "Our family is devastated."

Minjares and Deluna had been dating for about one year and had recently decided she would end their relationship, KHOU-TV reported.

A statement from Houston Professional Fire Fighters Association made no reference to the circumstances of Deluna's death, but said local firefighters were in mourning over the off-duty death.

"Our organization will strive to help support his brothers and sisters in the fire service, his family and his friends in this difficult time. Please keep his family and friends in your thoughts and prayers as answers are sought after this inexplicable tragedy," fire officials wrote to KPRC-TV.

Minjares, a nurse at Neighbors Emergency Center, leaves behind two daughters, ages 5 and 14.

Stacy Nigliazzo

Epitaph for a Young Woman
(a tanka)

Her love for her husband
was like saffron,
a spice made by grinding
a crocus's female sex organs
till just powder remains.

Jenna Le

Stay with Me Awhile

In this sea, we're all a band playing, a band drowning in the things that mattered: houses, walls, the pictures framed with bones. And then, the sky changes color. Wait a minute, baby. Where do you think you're going? Where do you think you matter? Fill your house with phones so you can call me anytime you want. Fill your house with plugs so you can recharge under the whirl of fan, crack of window, and stretch of book page. It only takes a moment. But now it's gone. Build around me. Build around my long hands that reach out to you, reach out for the things that don't matter anymore.

Loren Kleinman

After

I sat on the porch swing listening to the bees
praying in the lilacs. I thought of that scar

carved into her forehead. She told me
a box fell from a shelf in the garage.

I tried to remember what she said the day before.
She said, *he is sick*. She said, *leaving,* and

lawyers. She said, *unlucky,* and something
about not telling her mother. She never

said that she was scared.
She never said, *Restraining Order.*

If only I had had the chance I would have
given him the old *if you ever...again.* We

would have told everyone about him, built
a fortress with that knowledge.

I sat on the porch swing listening to the gospel of bees,
surveyed her life, then changed the ending.

Joy Gaines-Friedler

Leda Leaves Manhattan

Three days after it happened, I grab a greyhound
going west. All I have: a duffel stuffed with socks, t-shirts,
oil paints, a coffee-stained photo of my mother. A little cash.

I spark Marlboro menthols in the lavatory, spit smoke
into the no-flush toilet. Stench curls and thickens.
Fluorescents buzz overhead. The floor lurches beneath

my feet. Nothing is steady anymore. Door clicks shut;
I slump back to my window seat. I need to be landlocked,
waterless. I have friends in Kansas City. I'll crash

on couches, find some doctor to take care of me,
if it comes to that. I'll pursue a new hobby: take a shotgun
to the edge of a lake and shoot at every shadow of wings.

Emily Rose Cole

After Leaving Him

Such a gentle landing:
sun-filled kitchen,
pots and pans.

My children dance,
play games,
cuddle at bedtime.

Secrets spill from small throats.
We make a pact
never to see him again.

Lori Desrosiers

Peacemongering

Is it true that Frost wrote poems at night
in the kitchen with a revolver on the table next to him?
Uncomfortable with the truth that might come tumbling
unexpectedly from his words? Did be become impatient
with all the peacemongering? Do we all want, at some time,
to rise up fighting and turn words into bullets and give up
on prayer and plowshares, study and sacrifice
                    And like Frost
do we look and sound so predictable
and undangerous? Faithful farmers
watching fields of brown wheat and yellow corn,
pacing intensive care cubicles in isolation gown;
Walking through the green clearing,
caging free-range chickens, corralling colts,
holding back, fearful of great risk. Fearful of fields in flame.

                                        Judy Schaefer

The Sympathy of Dust

Her Hoover Vortex Master hums,
the house a diary of dross,
Pop-Tart crumbs, playground grit,
wicked grains of glass
the broom did not pick up
when her boyfriend broke
a long-neck PBR,
fragments of a narrative
she tracks from room to room,
cobwebs, dead bees, scented talc,
pollen shed by Easter lilies
one week past their prime,
and later when she cannot sleep,
the nightscape fills with cosmic dust
she heard Carl Sagan talk about
on the old Tonight Show,
comet ash and star-chaff
settling on her sleeping son
and on the now remembered face
of the whiskey-crippled father
she tried not to love,
how it falls, the dust of genesis,
until she falls asleep at last.

Edison Jennings

Calculatin

He got his nerve, walkin round with his head up like he tryin to
see pass the fog hangin over the Arkansas, his mouth shut tight like
a grasshopper jaws on a blade a wheat. He jes be actin cool like I
ain't got no right to know his business, shit. I ain't got no right to
do somethin bout the rips inside me raw as pig liver, ain't got no
right to ask him, Lord, what goin on? Can't say why, what for, how
long I gotta let him in the door like this, all stuck up like a cactus
somewhere in Texas jes fulla hisself, walkin through my words like
they some feathers come off his chest in this breeze blowin between
us, his coffee steamin like the tar bumps they been patchin up on the
street for bout a year now they ain't never gon get done an he keep
pourin more in, more steam and I was pleadin with that man tryin
to make him see what he done and Lord there was one time he was
tryin to be so righteous an God-a-mighty I woulda kill that man
if I'da been standin by the broom closet where I keep Mama iron,
somethin bigger than his hand hangin so casual like on his belt, but
it was hard to see, all them tears comin out my eyes, belly hurtin
somethin terrible, froze up in a scream so long on the inside. Don't
know if I coulda seen good-a-nough to kill a cockroach, I was shakin
an mad like a dog shut up a week an no water. I tell you girl I seen
something funny rise up in him, jes once, I could feel it twitchin that
colla I press on Saturday an I say to myself maybe he at leas gon say
he gon stop it, even if he can't say he sorry to his woman, so I try to
quit my shakin an my hand come out an then he got right up in my
face an he say *kiss my ass bitch.*

Well, the air stop and I lean back on my heels an then honey I jes
walk through that space like there wadn't nothin between us, no
name, no chile, no ford pickup, nothin, an I fill up the bucket,
swung out the mop an scrub that floor like I was raisin Lazarus an
I ain't once ask him what he done that for an I spit that soap over
my bare feet backa my knees an my behind an that the last time I
argue with that fool. He ain't getting no mo, neither. Cause I been
countin the things I need fa this life and that man don't figure.

Carol Barrett

Still Life with Road Kill

Spooled across the dirt road, the bear,
dead. A melodious spent planet.

I smelled its hold-your-breath,
kick-to-the-gut of life
stopped short. Whirring atop
its flattened skull's tire-track
tattoo, an unlucky wreath of flies.

I stood near the bear, hand
on chest. Not in some form
of prayer, but to press back
what had lain still.

I had a boyfriend who was struck by a car.
His death arrived like a gift.
I had wanted him to die.
His rage gobbled color,
blotted sound.

I thought of him afterwards
with a kind of shorthand:
Our legs beaded with lake water
His aversion to birds,
then beans. How good food
tasted when he wasn't there
to share it.

The bear was left on the road to rot.
It seemed undignified, the menace
reduced to a malingering mass.
Now I see the wisdom
in allowing its slow surrender.
Why bury what will never stay dead?

Tina Barry

Homeland

i come from still water lake
before sunrise.
searching for catfish saturday mornings.
if you don't catch 'em,
then you don't eat
is the joke my father forgets isn't funny
to grade school bellies gone empty to bed
more nights than anyone wants to remember.
this family is not for the faint of heart
because, yes,
two paychecks and decent neighbors
and church choir every sunday
but, large hands and closed minds turn
the best dads into beast men.

i come from hide
until you know it's a good day.
gauge the temperature of mother's prayers.
beg the baby to just be quiet
play outside and don't ask questions.
i come from *yes sir, no sir*
the rooms are clean
i won't make an noise
i stitched a meal from ketchup and rice
our brother is tending to the lawn work
mom is tattered pages of a wilting bible
held together with masking tape -
the words a poem that promises someday
something like God will be possible.
i come from possible
is friends who will give away
the things they trade for at lunch time.
miracles look like juice boxes
and quiet places to sleep;
from apology to relapse and sorry again;
from fear in all the wrong places.

i come from backyard barbeque
firefly lit the first day
pop comes home -
clean shirt, creased jeans and gift in hand
for all the days he was gone
and gone the days he was here.

daddy is a preacher now.
baby brother does not remember
the time when he wasn't.
mom is gratitude
sitting on the front porch
singing hymns to the still water
sunshine.

i come from still water
and broken promises,
from waiting for the other shoe to drop

Ashley Lumpkin

To the Girl Testifying About Her Assault at St. Paul's

I finally pulled the nasturtiums out of the too rich soil
in the planter. It was mid-July,
leaves the size of coasters but no blooms. I tossed
the uprooted plants on the driveway, too hot
to walk them all the way to the compost.
Days forgotten, from that heap
on the asphalt one morning
glowed three orange jewels.

Ann Quinn

Amen to All That

Can I be forgiven for imagining tire tracks across a black cassock, and shiny red studs in the tread of the tires? I heard he was flattened by a truck in Phoenix thirty years ago, when he stepped off the curb without looking. They say he was with the bishop. I imagine the two of them in their clerical garb, short stubby men, the bishop in his sash and beanie of episcopal purple, and his chunky amethyst ring the faithful were expected to kiss.

And I imagine beside the bishop on the corner that hot afternoon, that old priest, recently promoted to monsignor, sweating in his long black cassock, the red trim and sash identifying his somewhat lesser rank, and those red satin buttons neck to hem, shiny in the Arizona sun. Maybe he was blinded by the glare, distracted by a theological conversation perhaps, didn't hear the roar of fate rounding the corner, coming for him.

Martha K. Grant

Why Jesus Never Saved Me

tell me about the bishop, mother.
tell me how he pulled your organs
over
one by one

before he did it

tell me about the pew you sat in—
the mahogany in that wood

how he hovered his milk white drone
over your belly—

before he did it

tell me how he whispered
from a high point—*jesus will save you*
into your little girl ear

before he did it

tell me about the short migration
from your birth to this day
and break, little girl

tell me like talk story

tell me your body is old like language
in proximity to mine.

promise me that jesus didn't ask him
to savor little girls like wine.

Denise Benavides

Turnabout

Pound a pillow
my therapist says
pretend it's him

I pummel and punch
hitting back
till my arms grow tired

Try a silent yell
my therapist suggests
get it out

I scream without sound
till my throat burns

Imagine he's small
my therapist urges
the way you felt

I picture him shrunken
six inches high
a dictator doll
strutting on little feet
ranting in a tinny voice
shaking a tiny fist
till at last I laugh
and make him disappear

Joy Harold Helsing

Sunday Lunch

The others had left the clean-up to us,
and I trudged with catsup-smeared plates
from table to sink as my father whistled
and filled the dishwasher.
I wiped the table clear of runaway crumbs
and waited, as told, for him to finish.
Sunlight slipped past the front-yard elms, one shaft
of eerie light beaming through a window.

As my father reached for a towel
to dry his hands, I tried my exit.
Take out the trash before you leave, he said.
    I'll do it later.
Do it now, he said.
    No.

He turned from the sink, his mouth
shrunken into something like a hyphen,
a warning: *Do it now!*
and my thirteen-year-old feet stomped back
into the room towards the trashcan while he watched.

Now, do it with a smile on your face.

I stood straight, and silence flared.
    No.
His face pinched tighter, and he stepped towards me.
Stretching my lips clown-smile wide, I saluted,
hatcheting the air between us.
And he struck. He slammed me
against a cabinet, pinning my shoulders with his hands—
our faces just inches apart, each of us trying to recognize the other.

Elizabeth W. Jackson

Homecoming

The last time the colonel hit her,
she was sixteen. It was about the dishes
her brother should have washed
but didn't. They were sitting at the dinner table
on a Sunday, just finishing chicken and mashed potatoes,
green beans. Their father didn't care whose turn
it was. He just wanted them washed, and *now*.
He glared at her, like a gun barrel lowering.
And when she said *No, it's not my turn, I won't,*

he yelled, his eyes jittering into anger
that felt like shattering glass.
The rush of mountains closing in, a sense
of thunder. A force she dared resist so stupidly
that, when he hit her, she was still saying no,
and so, surprised. But he kept hitting,
took his belt off and walloped her
into a wailing so loud that, no longer caring,
she knew the neighbors heard.

Years later, flying back to the home never her home
after her father's stroke, and holding his hand
when he awoke from the coma and begged,
first, for his dog, and then, *please,* just take him home,
with her brother and sister-in-law fanning his face,
wiping away the sweat, at the end of his life
finally forgiving him his mortality, his failures:
the last words he spoke to them, the colonel,
their father, as he gazed up at them, hovering
around the narrow hospital bed, were

I have such good kids.

These words that passed for love.

Jane Chance

Ancestor Portrait

they say
my great-grandmother
was an acrobat
in a Chinese circus

i imagine her life
in the spotlight
a trained entertainer
made to follow orders
give a good performance

she was married off
to my great-grandfather
as second wife
breeding stock

shut in
after bearing children
i wonder what she thought
as she made her way
to the nearest bridge
and for her final act
leapt

without looking back

i hold
her limberness
in my limbs

her suicide
in my bones.

Angela Martinez Dy

In the Time of Scurvy

When brutality goes as far as brutality can – take it there, Killer –
brutality will be over, will have nothing left to prove, it bottoms
out, flattens, loses edge and dimension, bye-bye meaningful
concavity, farewell usable convexity, the for-real finish line, the
end right here at Ludlow's Smoker's Palace, a terminal terminal,
bringing humanity one step closer, brutality will not end alone, has
never operated in complete isolation, has required a recipient and
practitioner, two-in-one is fine, as long as there's an object of the
brutal gesture, so when brutality ends, other demises happen, like
clockwork till clockwork ends, a cascade of final moments, chain of
crescendos, till then, more transformations, more cycles, the rut of
change, gamut condition cities and shantytowns, my end in
the queue since I was born, but when it happens it means I've
become something which can end, a privilege, outlawed and
incomprehensible in the everlasting, I have not assumed a long
distance finish, with my killer, it will be personal, death craft, guild
worthy, up close details matter, increase, I see that irises in my
killer's eyes aren't solid, they are slit wheels, streaked, thin slices as
gray rays, gray rays as thin slices, wheels of fortune without need
to spin, I hope my killer hasn't been a ventriloquist before he kills
me, I hope he doesn't become one afterwards, if so, maybe he'll
be the last one, ventriloquism as far as it can go, no further, on his
knee, I still speak for me, last words, bloody tendrils, figure with
more than two sides, a story with only two sides seems so shallow,
nothing can drown in it, no room to dive safely, yet no danger
since the shallowness lacks challenge, lacks solidity's volume, which
isn't even a property of rock in all of rock's stages and ages, loose
in the volcano, all things molten except what has astronomical
melting point, no liver I know of, no lizard, definitely no lily, no
peak place to go once inside shallow, where go is all stretch without
exercise of dimension, no deep end but still invitations to drown,
no rising above the fusion of sky, ground, bras lift nothing, no
separation of church from state, smoke and blood pour into speech
bubbles, the 2D graphic life of taffy, just two measurements:
length, width, everything in a springy line, accommodated because
it could be flattened, the shadow knows, Mobius taffy, what does
this say about the substance of what can live there, the length of
forever, eventually, forever's substance might have to fold to fit,
might loop in having to cover infinity over and over, in the loop
there's emergence of dark spots, rope burn, friction, the stopping of
light has cast generalities, these stack up too, friction, a third

side begins to rise out of the flat single-celled ash, a mountain of soot, more sides, smoke-filled, misery-filled dreary little crystal, here comes tetrahedron, up, up emerges twelve-sided, twelve-tribed dodecahedron, peek at pyrite whose faces are not regular, no chin like my killer's, nothing like the military doctor Maj. Ishii Shiro, famous for biological experiments in Manchuria as profound as Mengele's, some say more, but in the realm of profundity at all, is there need to measure, the good fortune of a display of underthings of Marie Antoinette, including underhandedness related to the affair of the necklace, amazing, octahedral diamonds, replicas sliced into sequins, my shiny cheeks, what's left is all new moons, a day that is without its thong, the other names for singing are in the whorls, my fingertips contain circular music, concentric grooves on records played by tattoo needles, guillotine-edged diamond stylus, rivulets of my blood thin as hair, longer than hair so many men prefer, whether or not they are killers, a length some might kill for, longplaying album, delight of diamond cutters, steady tone arm, so as not to skip a beating, my killer's name becomes the name of death like mine exactly, the name of method, even before it happens, I'm in the early stages of conceit that my murder has such power, is innovation documented in the annals, books with a taste for the truest crime spare no detail, comprehensive condemnation contains also the full text of justification for praise, prizes for reporting, links to the Starr report, legitimate history that my killer reads, bedtime story, once upon a time there was a trollop, on the occasion of the negligee, the man takes it off of her, her willing lover, his willing lover, reciprocal actions, of course, unwilling lover: this dominates, is required; throws it on the floor, big woo, big deal, except that he strangles me with it, à la heroics of the Boston strangler, critically acclaimed movie, many more since, soon enough, one about me, best picture of the year, best actor portrays a serial killer, I know the dialogue by heart, answer to Clarice, except that in slow motion, there is descent like skin of hands detaching from dead bodies bloating in rivers and lakes, in storm and sewage drainage systems, not far from here, skin of hands detaching like gloves coming off at the end of some kind of elegance, snapshot, the absolute end of elegance =

Thylias Moss

The Matchsticks I Sold for Him

His camera must be balanced on the railing, timer set
to catch us frozen in half-light, stilled by his tongue,
a different us captured on the faded surface, rounded
corners, yellowed under the film, the us who lived
that distant, disappearing life. The camera wobbled.
He held out his hands, palms up, placating to stabilize,
ran to join me, wrapped his arm around my waist, steadying
before the ticking of the timer stopped. It stopped,
like the falling yellow leaves, the creek that babbled,
the spring of rusty waters once bottled for the ailing
who sought any curative, any snake oil, any hope.
The photos stick together now, the way memory
clings, bleeds colors and time, the way flames blur
a cacophony, like the weight of his hand on my hip.

Laura Madeline Wiseman
& Andrea Blythe

brothers with dreadlocks will kill you too

we sat glazed translucent slicing our love into thick rings
like onions for stew or soup we pretended we weren't
earthbound king queen of too many dramas that left me
wandering alone picking flowers that had no smell whose
blossoms did not die wilt bleed beneath strangulations
we grew fond of the toxins breeding beneath our pillows
confessions that shake hair skin loose shed memories like
childhood diseases i am not a man to use my hands for
anything but pleasure art praise i will not walk these streets
for a job it always led back to this conversation money for
the rent the electricity i wanted to walk with him all the
way to his country to his blind grandmother her herd of
goats his uncles backs scorched in banana fields i wanted to
run with him in a field of blossoms that would bend under
our feet but he could not go back to the ghosts that had
learned how to pick the locks on his grandmothers doors
instead they followed learned the languages of a thousand
borders they watch us from the bowl of mangoes crawl
through our dirty laundry scratch their teeth on the last fifty
dollar hidden beneath my socks a feast of blood he wrote
across the mirrors throughout the house a feast of words
red pink orange blush gold lipsticks broken smeared listen
to me his eyes cried my mouth is out of order my spirit
drags me rises to the top of the ceiling a room of pleasure
i discover a new cobalt in the moroccan rugs reflections
of my still hands mesmerize inlaid mirrors turkish tea trays
overturned wooden bracelets dangling silver bells sparkling
light witness red silk bedspread waiting for my hair to spill
spread antique sari curtains stained by my blood books
journals prayer beads a womb field of lavender his dreads
soaking my blood his fingers removing the pearl necklace
from the carved bedpost a gift for the daughter i will
never meet now as his feet explode inside his head his pee
rattling like yellow rain my last breath finds a hole inside
his coat pocket i crawl inside listen to his heart write beat
escape wipe the splattered blood from his undying love
confession our lips remember this unspoken death our
home remembers windowsills of lavender peasant bread
papaya salsa mint baths rosemary mornings two mounds
of red earth where elders wail stoop to listen to the crone
who sells fish in the market her breath stinking truth into
chastising i no cry for the young lions what you mean you
think him no kill she.

Jaki Shelton Green

Sagittarius

I.

longing and fire
December waters
tourmaline
smudged silver leaf
down waterfall hill the dogs bark
chase the archer
who fights restriction
who fragments in scatters
she survived the bathtub
by dint of who she is
little winter fled
July's dripping lion mouth
her baby woman parts
shielded by salvia
the water's red rust
its blooms
haunt her adult bed
in spasms and soft masses
Born into viridian
she rages carmine

II.

The fifteenth year of absence
I fill a bowl with water
to call the creek
at Middle White Oak
and sip the heat
of African Nectar.
This day long ago
bone thin head
a smudge
beneath my rib cage
cheek, forehead
mouse child
seashell and fingernail
she swam with every
egg nested in
my womb's antlers
I swam with every egg
of my long-gone mother

III.

she manufactured selves
and threw them behind her
jackrocks to stymie
the ravenous big tires
the blood red exhalation
burning smudge of sage
can not safeguard the little mother
she was under the waterfall
and the babies
knowing her ground
holding her ground
and the babies
holding her entire
the little mother
withstands
fists in a bus stop
underground
she invented a quilt
pulled up to her seashell ear
and made the outside babies
babies who came from the carnelian
of her
from her rusted
intransigent fracture

Faith S. Holsaert

[note: Jackrocks: Striking coal miners in WV weld metal spikes into a shape like the child's toy, but so large that when thrown in the path of a coal truck, the tires will be punctured and the truck halted.]

Daphne

It is better not to have a body.
In the forest, sun on leaves,
small animals scurrying, a soft "coo"
in the trees. And the footfalls, closer, closer.
I can feel the sharp male eyes.
I streak my face with mud
and let the north wind
whip my hair to knots.
Perhaps the skin of deer can hide my rounding hips.
Beauty is a wound.

Each day I train, trying to grow faster.
Each night, the hideous whisper of love.
I bound over moss and twigs, running
like a hare beneath the stark moon's icy light.
No child can escape a god.
The fingers reach for me.
Better not to have a woman's body.
When there is nothing, there is prayer.

Alison Stone

Sufferance

Transgender, as in counterfeit, as in someone *appearing*
or *attempting to be* a member

of the other gender, as in equated with *transsexual*
or *cross-dresser* or *pervert*

as in *a term used by ugly girls as a defense mechanism
against prettier girls.* As in

the only solution lies in psychology or religion or,
until 1960, an icepick lobotomy

done without drugs. Sufferance means *passive permission
from lack of interference,*

as in *tolerance* of something intolerable, the teen set on fire
at the back of the bus, the way the world

daily scathes you, my fear for your safety a daily sufferance,
as in *endurance,* as in [archaic] *misery,*

as in Middle English or Latin equivalent of *suffer,* akin
in its way to *suffrage,*

the right to vote. As in vote for, support—child, I am trying
to support you in this—

as in *Ecclesiastical,* a prayer, an *intercessory prayer or petition.*
Intercessory, come between.

Intercede, yes—my body—between yours and theirs.

Rebecca Foust

Working definitions in this poem are from dictionary.com and urbandictionary.com

Julia Tells Me About Her Summer
While Installing Her New Chandelier

A man felt her up, so she took his picture:
a scowling face, a big hand in the flash.
Police weren't interested. Her passing body
had been grazed, they said, that's all: grazed
as grass is grazed by animals. *Fuck off.*
She called the Post Intelligencer. That night
they posted it online. And all that night
emails piled up, their lines rang off
the hook—*a story's broke,* they said, *a flash
flood.* Turned out he had a record, grazed
and leaned against a lot downtown women.
Who could have IDed him? *Nobody,*
the police said. But plenty did. Somebody
called the News. It should be safe at night,
one reporter said. The man still gazed,
bleary and mad, inside the picture.
Been on parole, a reporter found. *Flash
Alert* played Julia's call, her soft "fuck off"—
a DJ sampled it. The man was taken off
the streets. *So, I got free shit from everybody
downtown. Ryler, my business took off.* The flash
of fame is why, I realized, earlier tonight,
our server said she was a hero. *Picture
that!* She laughs. *Like my ex, grazed
by that bullet in pursuit, pepper-sprayed, and tased
while in his superhero suit, off
fighting "crime," live-tweeting all those pictures
of his abs in training. What a body!
But what a loco bastard. The real Dark Knight!*
We laugh together. Passing headlights flash
against her chandelier—fake diamonds flash
on glass arms, bright as fish that graze
out past the skiffs, where it's always night.
We watched a video of them, once. The drop off
falls away for miles. Their soft bodies
withstand five hundred tons. Our only pictures
come from submarine—night-pictures
of aliens grazing on darkness, bodies blazing.
Jules checks her work. It flashes on and off.

Ryler Dustin

Off

He's off, he's really off, he's so far off
he'll never come down, been off for a
week now, no, two weeks, the water's
deep, he's so far gone he'll never come
up, he'll probably be off the rest his life,
off to Omega and no insurance.

I'm off too, she said. Outtahere–off,
if he comes home oiled again. Get off
of me, she said, I mean if a man is going
to act like that, I'm gone, away, off the
shelf, absentee, off before you off me
off like a sock, you're off your rocker,
you know that? Off your nut. Off
your trolley, call 911.

That's way off, he said, just because
I'm off the wagon doesn't mean I don't
love you no more. Oh yeah, she said,
Oh yeah, he said, and he took off
his shirt and cuffed her.

I'm off, she said, I'm really off,
and she should have gone, she
should have gone.

Lois Marie Harrod

The Man in Miami

Sometimes my sister calls to say
she's seen that man again
following fifty feet behind her on the street,
hiding his head when she looks, or
sitting only a few café tables away
pretending to read, or
pacing in his camouflage jacket
outside her window.
Other times she hasn't seen him
in a day. What am I supposed to say?
Walk a different way to work,
stay with a friend, call the police,
come home?
I've said it all; the man won't go.

It doesn't snow where my sister lives,
and it's always two hours later.
Here the days are cold. It grows dark
earlier each evening. When she calls
it is twenty years ago and she has slipped
into my room. She nudges me awake;
she whispers in my ear:
it is our grandfather come for a visit,
it is our grandfather waiting
by the stairs. I used to look.
There was never anyone there.

My sister says: that doesn't matter.
That doesn't matter at all. What matters
is that crazy man who will not let me alone.

She does not know how long
the man has followed her.
Six weeks, or eight?
He sat on the hood of her car
in his camo jacket and black sunglasses.
He nodded, as if to say hello,
then rose and ambled down the busy street.

As a girl, she saw many things
that were not there: Birds
circling above her bed, and, later,
tiny figures swinging from the curtains.
Sometimes it was some kind of devil
rocking on his hooves
over by the bedroom door. Our mother
took her to the doctor, who told her:
these things aren't real; they can't hurt you.
Sleep with the lights on.

Here, it won't stop snowing.
Each evening, everything is buried again,
and the icicles are heavier.
The man in Miami hasn't touched her,
so no one can do a thing.
If he doesn't touch her, no one can know a thing.

Kevin Prufer

Maya, meaning *the invincible*

The woman retreating grows steadily darker. Retreating, the woman grows steadily darker. Darker, the woman steadily retreating grows. Darker, the woman retreating steadily grows. Darker and darker. Retreating, retreating. To disappear is the most difficult and darkest thing. The dearest thing, to be dark and visible. I will her dear and dark. Visible and unwrecked. Last week, another woman was yanked from her car for dark. Leaving this woman I love's hometown for her now-home. Where I love her. From where she is retreating. Yanked from a car for failure to signal. For failure to silent. Her name is Sandra and she is dead. Maya is not dead, will not dead. I say it to believe it. Maya is retreating. To the place where the woman dead. I nothing here. I say only not dead. Unwrecked. Say it toward the retreating. Steady. Not dead. Dark and visible. Dark and not dead. Not wrecked. Dark and living. Bright and living. Growing dark and steady, very alive.

Marty McConnell

Every Time You Write About Marissa Alexander

you end up on vacation.

Every time you write about Marissa Alexander, you start at the same place:
Marissa Alexander's packing her clothes. Rico Gray comes in, gets in her face.
I'm going to kill you, bitch! he screams through the bathroom door.

You're on vacation.

You're on vacation with your family.
You're nine or ten or twelve-years-old staring at the same red carpet
    the same red walls
Same air-conditioner chilling in the window humming through it all.
Your father stands tall announcing, *Today, you're going to shoot a gun.*

You're on vacation.

Marissa Alexander is able to get to the garage, but automatic door won't engage.
Rico Gray is flying though rage. *I'm going to kill you, bitch!* The door won't open.
Marissa Alexander goes to the glove box and grabs her gun.

You're at the gun range.

You're at the gun range and you're holding a .38
police special – the weight of it holds your whole body down.
It's the lightest gun you can find.
White man comes up from behind
puts his hands over yours saying *Let me help you, son.*

Daughter.
Marissa Alexander just had a daughter.
Preemie. 8 months.
She aims for the wall.

The White man who's not your father at all
says *Let me help you, son*
and wraps his hands around yours so that
 it's his hands and the gun
and your hands are no more. You have White-man hands
holding a .38 special flat nose enclosed base.
Hold it steady hold it straight.
Shoot for the black face.

The tin target
the smiling face:
two dots and a curve
scorched dark from a thousand sparks
a thousand shots
a thousand vacationers that come and go
face still smiling though

still saying *C'mon brother, come take a shot*
I dare you. I double dog dare you.
Come point your gun and have a nice day.

Rico Gray
says *If I can't have you, no one will*
flies into rage and threatens to kill
has five baby-mamas and beat every last one.
Marissa Alexander cocks the gun.

You pull the trigger.

Quincy Scott Jones

Courthouse

At the rally for the woman who was raped
by that cop, Reverend Billy started in on
corporations, eventually winding his way down
to her body. The booing stopped, then. In Bushwick,
near Varet Street, one wheat pasted sign reads
you can't have capitalism without racism and another
says occupy my penis. Audre Lorde said *the master's tools
will never dismantle the master's house* which I hated
when I first heard it – of course plantation tools
could kick holes in walls, of course fire burns both
fields and hearths, until I realized what she meant.
Or maybe I still don't. Maybe the sign should have read
you can't have capitalism without misogyny or plain old *fuck cops* –
after the trial was over, a jury member said, of course
the cop did it, we just didn't have enough to convict. It was
he said she said. Here's all I can say: the cops formed
a wall outside the courthouse, hands behind their
backs, chests forward. Like they were the ones under
attack. Like it's not violence if someone gets off.

Monica Wendel

Dear Police Officer,

Please. Let me explain. No, I won't lie. Yes, I knew very well that time was expiring on the meter in the street below, where my old car sat parked, the car you were slowly circling. But I couldn't leave, you see. Sonia Sanchez was reading and Max Roach was resurrected and I was sitting between two poet-friends and we knew we weren't going anywhere as she continued to hum long after her scheduled hour was up, and she was telling us to move to that pulpit, you see, encouraging us to be bold, to turn and face the scorn and frowns of the men and women, the strangers and friends, who will never welcome us back, urging us to find a way to say what needs to be said, to gain the courage to act no matter what one's culture, color, creed, no matter what one's gender, race, religion, no matter by what other ways and means we humans are so arbitrarily divided, and there she was calling to us, to me, to be brave, me, a woman who had hoped to learn the art of audacity by now, and time is running out, don't you see? Always running out, and sometimes we have to ignore meters running over, and she and Max began to blend as one and their rhythms began to fuse and she was moving between singing and speaking, speaking and singing, and so please forgive me, officer, as I will forgive my town, my countries, my parents, myself, my old life and new, the history that is mine and the history that is not, and (maybe) even those who refuse to raise the minimum wage, but I refuse to hold my tongue any longer, and I'm going to stand on that pulpit, find the courage to speak loud and long, so please, officer, tell me you will see this as case dismissed, close your yellow notebook, tuck it back into your pocket, and then shake your head a little as you walk away, crossing the street, patting the notebook, nodding a little as you say, yes, I get it. Yes, I do believe I get it.

Andrea Witzke Slot

They Will [Not] Speak Of

The women will not speak when they speak,
they will speak of *that time*. When they speak,
wiping hands on apron checks, they will not
speak of *what mustn't be named*. One might
say *that time* while pounding out dough and men
will stroke graying beards in a living room
laden with apples and pine, girls with down
cast eyes. They'll say *we didn't tell her
because*. They'll say *it's better she not know*.
Insert your horror here [   ]. It was years ago.

Silence grows louder, ever outward:
*We thought she was making it up
to hide an affair,* those grass stains on
her nightdress (unable to lift arms
in protest), dirt clods in her bed.
What was once quiet pasture becomes
voices shushed in latticed pie crusts.
That's all behind us now, the civic
leader rings out, naming it *wild female
imaginings*. It's still happening.

They will speak of forgiveness. They will not
say *violence*. The minister comes round,
tall hat bobbing, speech not a rhapsody
but could be. *God chooses his people
with tests of fire.* She is milking a cow
when he says this, aware of heat friction
fingers chafe over chapped nipples.
She won't look at him. *If you won't forgive God
can't forgive you.* The shaking woman
rocks back and forth and says *I forgive him*.

Ellen Kombiyil

It's OK to Say These Things

Wood
        Shell

                Bone

                      Buttons

in every size and color
        your mother saved for mending.
           You saved them, too,

in the gleaming tin on a high shelf.
        Snowy days, and you'd take it down
           and we'd remember

buttons from faded summer dresses,
        buttons from coats returned from war,
           buttons with bits of garments still clinging,

           flesh and tendon of them.

Red grosgrain, shock of silver wedding silk,
        fingers of fragrance still clinging.
           Attar of rose and vetiver still clinging.

Heft and pour, the cascading clack and clatter
        of buttons, like coins or pretend jewels.
           You, too, loved them. You and I together

breathed the old secrets hanging
        like the kitchen smells
           of your Bronx apartment.

Buttons from a man's flannel before zippers were.
        Your father's, you said, and the blue bruise
           your mother tried to hide with a lock of hair when

you, looking, and in your small voice asked,
What happened to your eye, Mama?
as she reattached the right arm of your school sweater.

The bleats of a skinny infant rose in the next room,
and a darkness you hoisted onto your eight-year-old hip
and hauled through the rest of your life.

Hauled it into my life, too.

Would you believe me if I told you I survived your winter?
Here is the faith I've entered with myself,
rule, rite, and rigor of it:

I will not belong
to whatever happens to me.
It's OK to say these things.

Maria Rouphall

My Stepmother Takes Me to the Fair

Give me again your upturned wrists that night
at the Tennessee Valley fair. Our green car wheeled
over knotted crowds and lakes, the Midway

a sequined collar, carnies' shout: *guess your weight,*
your weight for a quarter. Swoop and twitter of bullbats,
our world topsy, the Scrambler twirled like sugary scarves

in the cotton candy machine. Now our heads thrown
back, wrist to wrist under the canopy, grinding
the last of September into sawdust. We could live

in the straw with the prize lambs, crawl down
the calliope pipes, travel to Chicago with the Bearded
Lady. I could leave my brother alone in the crib,

my mother's house of mirrors I stumble through.
Foaming out of the hallway, she and my stepfather
naked, rank with beer, her head slammed in the wall

like a ball at the stacked bottles rigged to never
collapse, never win a rhinestone hat or bowl of goldfish.
Turn the whites of your wrists to me again, spin off

higher than anyone can see, drunk in the seat
of big-shouldered trees, burst of chrysanthemums
pounding our hair and surrendered faces.

Linda Parsons

You Didn't Do Anything

"I think we win, by surviving."
— Courtney Kendall

You had reached the age when these things
happen, a freshman in college, homesick
your teeth soft, your mouth cherry bright

You watched the after school specials
their watered down wisdom promising to prepare you
for this: your violent moment of fame

Remember how it felt familiar?
Even as your mind fluttered through
its blank reel of film, even as you

dreamed escape routes, your body all
run and struggle, fighting, as you sat shock still,
his hands an exclamation at your throat.

Whatever it was, it was enough,
an undeserved inheritance, the color
of your grief, deep yellow at your bedside

You do not need to prove it, how
our language stumbles and stops
short, unable to articulate his tender

brutality, how a love like terror felt
safe, how a love like that felt deserved.
Let this be your deposition, your oath,

palm pressed to your breast, swear
it on the body you dug up from the grave
You didn't do anything wrong, you

didn't do anything, only nineteen
and green, your shoots pushing back
against these confines of soil and stone

Watch, as you expand, unrepentant, your smile
wide and sharp, your lips snapped tight,
hungry for what only you can devour.

Jessica Lohafer

Minding My Business

I was at a club one night for a benefit:
Amnesty International, a cause anyone would support.
Shake a bucket on the corner, dollars will drop in.
We were dancing with our feet and signing postcards
with both hands: South Africa, Chile, Bulgaria.
They had a raffle with the cards and I won
four free tanning sessions. Wonderful. I gave it away,
thinking *Hell of a prize for Amnesty:* Laos, Nigeria.
Leaving the bar, grateful for fresh, quiet air,
I unlocked my bike slowly, giving another woman
I didn't know a chance to get in her car. This intersection
is dangerous: Brazil, El Salvador. I was fiddling
with my helmet when a man came up and asked the driver
for a ride. She hesitated. I shook my head behind his back.
He wheedled *Pretty-please.* She, unsure, looked at me.
She doesn't want to give you a ride, I said. *Please leave her alone.*
She drove away, and he spun on me. *Just you mind your business!*
The world would suck if everyone did that, I shouted,
moving away, thinking Paraguay, Syria, Cambodia.
Come over here and I'll suck . . . but why repeat it?
All I hear is Paraguay, Syria, Cambodia, and you.

Tracy Mishkin

Phoenix

I'm awake in this bed on a school night and it is 3:42 a.m.
I am not asleep because I found a vice in caffeine.
So I brace myself against the back of the person I'm lying in this bed
with for support while I think.

7 years old
The game "daddy chase Aleenah around the house, catch her and
body slam her onto the couch" got me 3 stitches and a dinosaur
band-aid that wore my face like a champ!

    Note: Banging my head against a wall wasn't always on purpose.

13
A girl tells me my scar is ugly.
She says she can cut me some bangs.
This is the 1st time I changed myself for someone else.

10
I ask the girl down the street, "Do you want to be my friend?"
She says yes.

20
I ask the girl in my lecture hall, "Do you want to be my friend?"
She says no.

18
I tell a man "I love you"
He doesn't say the same words back

19
A chocolate lab lifts his leg on my chest and marks me as his territory

20
A man asks me to be his girlfriend.
I tell him, "I'm already another dogs property, why would I want to
be yours too?"
He calls me a bitch.

16

The phrase "loose lips" quickly becomes interchangeable with
the word "whore" after confiding in my best friend that I lost my
virginity after I said no.

20

After reading my rape poem to a roomful of strangers, a woman
comes up to me and thanks me for telling our story so well.
I tell her,
"Rape does not define you."

20 ½

Feeling mature, I finally take my own advice.

> Fact: Being a black, female, college student who was previously
> raped once before, statistically makes it impossible NOT to be
> raped again.

21

If you say no and are forced to have sex after midnight on New
Year's Eve do you have to take "not being a statistic" off of your
resolution list?

21

I am 10 times more likely to be raped a 3rd time than I am to get in
a car accident.
So I throw all this baggage in my car, drive around TX for 8 hours
and end up unpacking everything into my mother's chest. Jesus
that woman carries such a heavy heart for me.

> Note: It is exhausting to hear myself talk about this so often.
> Note: It is discouraging that rape manifests itself in my poetry.
> Note to self: If I'm not happy on paper, am I truly happy in person?

21

At a bar, a woman I have never met tells me her own story.
I am an open heart.
She hugs me and says,
"Rape does not define you."

6 ½ years old

While arguing with my father, he stops right in the middle of all
the tears and smiles.

He says, "Always stick up for yourself knucklehead, be confident in
what you believe in."

> Note: When arguing with my father nowadays, I can see that
> he almost regrets ever telling me that.

So to that girl in my lecture hall that didn't want to be my friend,
the girl that said my scar was ugly, the man who never said I
love you back, the two men that I never let beat me and most
importantly to myself:

Stop.

You have got to get the fuck over yourself to get up and unchain that
ego that is weighing on your ankles. Look around and breathe it all in.
The world is not a shitty place filled with shitty people.

We all still have simple childhood perceptions, we're just "used to
what we see"

It's all taken for granted.

Granted,

I think my bangs are pretty dope and most recently I don't think
anyone should be frugal with the word LOVE.

But I digress.

So it's now 4:43 am. I'm still awake and wired on caffeine. Time is
still moving. And everything in the past has passed.

So...

Hi,

My name is Aleenah. I've only been alive 23 years now, but I think
I still got a few more left in me.

> Do you want to be my friend?

Aleenah Spencer

Arboreal

Above the roofline of my mother's house I am
a child holding tight to the arms of the old maple,
it was a sapling in that spot before
I ever breathed, or anyone in my family.
Its trembly gray-barked branches often ladder
my weight into the unwritten notes of the wind—
this day the rush of its fingers loosens my braid
wild dark hair swaying,
my whole body sways at the crest
of that tree, that womb of leaves and branches.
        Together we become music,
        I breathe the smell fresh as sunlight,
        a song nesting at the back of my throat,
        this moment more important:
        the wilderness of my heaven,
than every secret in the house below—
        My thin frame a reed in that canopy.

Kathrine Cays

Build a cello

Build a cello in which to live,
an instrument whose harmonics
make you a hymn to guardians,
forty thousand of them yearning
for your ear after millennia
of ancestral meddling—savages

interfering with you in bed,
rearranging the furnishings
of your head to mislead you
in your mistakes. And then,
praying with sharpened stone,
a shaman to yourself, you cut

the milky way connecting you
to your delusions and bow
the strings of your new dwelling
across the bridges of the mind
as if you were born deserving it
and the world had sung alleluia.

Djelloul Marbrook

Persephone

Persephone,
you left your violets
in the shade of a
mesquite.

Weeping blood,
a horned toad
watches them wilt.

When winter comes,
even the canyons moan
your absence.

Chris Wise

Sirens

Say someone will come,
but no one comes. The echo

filters through buildings. Palm fronds
feather tile and stone,
                    yet I remember

only mountains. Snow circling our house
like crows' wings. How I long for cold

metal stinging my hands. I had
a mother then. I held the wind
in my throat like a song. A coal-

black sky, blue-lit by morning
that arrives too late somewhere
north. I lay down on the bed to sirens

            like a loon's calls. Like blood. The torn pocket
            of skin dangling where the blade exited

my mother's back. Each staple
making a new hole. Tonight,
no one comes
                    with sounds that carry, with water
that will tumble from the sky. That starved town
in the distance is the gash

where she was torn from
breast plate to shoulder

blade. If I could unzip cold
skin, maybe I'd know
how to stop reaching

            for snow, dark blue
            mountains haloed by stars.

Chelsea Dingman

In a Deep Pool Bound by Cement

In a deep pool bound by cement,
in water black as the Exxon oil slick,
my daughter and I swim. Thick scum trails our arms
like moss, and fish bump and touch our legs
like caresses from childhood.
We'd better get out, I say, and she nods, her arms strong,
her stroke sure. We are both calm
in spite of chill currents and the inky meniscus.
More afraid than she is (I think now on looking back),
I break the surface first and pull myself
onto the wall. *Hurry,* I suggest,
my tone light, my hand reaching for hers
over water so dense there's no reflection.
She swims slowly, blonde hair wet only at the tips,
a dark fringe dipping and rising.
Her body is incandescent as a nocturnal beetle,
and yet utterly human. Then she too pulls herself up,
towels off, and joins me on the rim.

Cortney Davis

The Voices of Women

I was listening to the voices of women
who cried out in many tongues,
many of them reduced to

the unique inverted,
the head upside down through the habit
of being trained in dressage,

I thought it was you who put down the innocent,
I thought I was only floating when guilty,
on the stained floor of the kitchen,

and it was not enough
cooked in the bone marrow and small bags,
who gave of vinegar and oil,

who were consumed by a cruelest of bread, who was meek
and not inherited, who was a peacemaker
who found a cold shoulder, turning,

always turning away into
someone else's morning, who
hungered and thirsted for the scent of orange blossoms

and who was kept like muscle weakness
in a cage for growing calves, pure
of heart and met by the proscriptions of a parakeet

exercising its rules by rote, who was merciful
and told to gnaw on a borrow of soap, who was
hungry and thirsty and cried out I love you to an empty

electronic ear, who writhed in the forsakenness
of the body, who was taken for speaking the wrong
language and shipped back to

what owned her, while her children that no one understood
cried out in their new homeland of orphanages
until, abruptly and

inexplicably, as a star turning
on its axis, the human voice broke free of the chord
of deafness

into nothing but joy

Rebecca Seiferle

Biographies & Acknowledgements

Leila Allen is a middle grades teacher in Swannanoa, North Carolina where her curriculum has heavy emphasis on banned books, Shakespeare, and poetry of all kinds. Leila lives with her husband, two sons, step-daughter, and an absurd number of cats. She is also a rape survivor.

E. Kristin Anderson is a poet and author living in Austin, TX. She is the co-editor of *Dear Teen Me,* an anthology based on the popular website and her next anthology, *Hysteria: Writing the female body,* is forthcoming from Sable Books. She is currently curating *Come as You Are,* an anthology of writing on 90s pop culture for ELJ Publications. Kristin is the author of eight chapbooks of poetry including *A Guide for the Practical Abductee* (Red Bird Chapbooks), *Pray, Pray, Pray: Poems I wrote to Prince in the middle of the night* (Porkbelly Press), *Fire in the Sky* (Grey Book Press), *She Witnesses* (dancing girl press), and *We're Doing Witchcraft* (Hermeneutic Chaos Press). Kristin recently took a position as Special Projects Manager for ELJ and is a poetry editor at *Found Poetry Review.* Once upon a time she worked at *The New Yorker.*

Shawn Aveningo is an award-winning, globally published poet whose work has appeared in over 100 literary journals and anthologies, including LA's *poeticdiversity* who recently nominated her poetry for a Pushcart Prize. She is co-founder of The Poetry Box®, managing editor of *The Poeming Pigeon* and board member and website designer for *VoiceCatcher.* Shawn's a proud mother of three and lives in Beaverton, Oregon with her husband. She believes poetry is the perfect literary art form for today's fast-paced world, due to its power to stir emotion in less than two minutes. An earlier version of "The Day I Saw My Rapist at the Corner Texaco" was published by *Heart Journal* in January, 2015.

Carol Barrett holds doctorates in both clinical psychology and creative writing. She is the recipient of an NEA fellowship in poetry, and has published poetry in numerous magazines and anthologies, including The Women's Review of Books, Feminist Studies, Bridges: A Journal for Jewish Feminists and Our Friends, JAMA (Journal of the American Medical Association) and Poetry International. Her book *Calling in the Bones* won the Snyder Prize from Ashland Poetry Press (2005). Carol teaches for Union Institute & University and for Saybrook University. "Calculatin" was first published in the 1992 Crossing Press anthology *What's a Nice Girl Like You Doing in a Relationship Like This? Women in Abusive Relationships,* edited by Kay Marie Porterfield.

Tina Barry's poems and short stories have been published widely in various journals including *Drunken Boat,* and *Veils, Halos & Shackles, International Poetry on the Oppression and Empowerment of Women* (Kasva Press). Two pieces in *Mall Flower,* her first book of poems and short fiction (Big Table Publishing, 2015), were nominated for the Pushcart Prize. Her story "Going South" will appear in *The Best Small Fictions 2016* (Queens Ferry Press, October 2016).

Zeina Hashem Beck is a Lebanese poet. Her first collection, *To Live in Autumn,* won the 2013 Backwaters Prize. She's also the author of two chapbooks: *3arabi Song* (2016), winner of the 2016 Rattle Chapbook Prize, and *There Was and How Much There Was* (2016), a smith|doorstop Laureate's Choice, selected by Carol Ann Duffy. Her work has been nominated for the Pushcart Prize, Best of the Net, and the Forward Prize, and has appeared in *Ploughshares, Poetry Northwest,* and *The Rialto,* among others. She lives with her husband and two daughters in Dubai, where she has founded and runs PUNCH, a poetry and open mic collective. Zeina is a strong performer of her poetry, and has participated in literary festivals in the Middle East, the UK, and the US.

Shaindel Beers is the author of two full-length poetry collections, *A Brief History of Time* (2009) and *The Children's War and Other Poems* (2013), both from Salt Publishing. She is currently the chairperson of the English Department at Blue Mountain Community College in Pendleton, Oregon, and serves as Poetry editor of *Contrary Magazine.*

For first generation Chicana poet, **Denise Benavides**, writing has become a haven for growth, for understanding, and immortalizing life's humanness. Currently living in Oakland, CA as an emerging poet and performer, her work has been published in *FatCity Review, Ground Protest Poetry, The Far East: Everything As It Is,* and *The Acorn Review.* She is currently working on her upcoming collection of poetry titled: *There Are No Safe Words Here.*

Shavawn M. Berry's poetry has appeared in *Poet Lore, Olentangy Review, Black Fox Literary Magazine, The Huffington Post (Huffpo 50), The Cancer Poetry Project 2, Rebelle Society, Meridian Anthology of Contemporary Poetry, Westview – A Journal of Western Oklahoma, The Bellingham Bay Monthly, Synapse, Blue Mountain Arts/SPS, Poetry Seattle,* and *Lead Stone.* Her prose has been published by *Be You Media Group, Rebelle Society, elephant journal, The Good Men Project, Vagina – The Zine, North Atlantic Review, Concho River Review, addictionsolutions.com, buddhajones.com, Living Buddhism,* and *The World Tribune,* to name a few.

As a member of Slam Richmond, **Casandra Faith Broaddus** helped her poetry slam team to place 8th in the nation at the 2012 National Poetry Slam. Currently, the writer and performer is teaching English and creative writing and serves as a journalist in the US Army Reserve. Her poem "War on Women" has been previously published in Write Bloody Publishing's *We Will Be Shelter: Poems for Survival* (10 Dec 2014), and a performance has been featured on Button Poetry.

Sivan Butler-Rotholz is the editor of the Saturday Poetry Series on As It Ought To Be and the founder of Reviving Herstory. Her poetry, nonfiction, and original comics appear online and in print. A recovering attorney, she earned her MFA from Brooklyn College and is working on her debut novel. Sivan lives in the 6th borough of NYC with her husband and their young son.

Andrea Blythe writes speculative poetry and fiction, which has appeared in various publications. Her first chapbook of poetry, *Pantheon,* is forthcoming from ELJ Publications in August 2017.

Hélène Cardona is a poet, literary translator and actor, the recipient of numerous awards and honors including a Hemingway Grant and the USA Best Book Award. Her books include three poetry collections, most recently *Life in Suspension* and *Dreaming My Animal Selves* (Salmon Poetry); and three translations: *Beyond Elsewhere* (White Pine Press), *Ce que nous portons* (by Dorianne Laux, Éditions du Cygne), and *Walt Whitman's Civil War Writings* for *Whitman-Web.* She contributes essays to *The London Magazine* and co-edits *Plume Journal* and *Fulcrum: An Anthology of Poetry and Aesthetics.* She holds a Master's in American Literature from the Sorbonne, and taught at Hamilton College & Loyola Marymount University. Hélène had roles in *Chocolat, Jurassic World, The Hundred-Foot Journey, Dawn of the Planet of the Apes, Serendipity,* and *Mumford.* "Requiem for a Shark" was first published in *Near Kin: A Collection of Words and Art Inspired by Octavia Estelle Butler* (Sybaritic Press).

Kathrine Cays is a multimedia artist/writer who was born in the Appalachian Mountains of Pennsylvania. Kat received her Bachelor of Arts degree in Studio Art and Creative Writing at the University of North Carolina at Chapel Hill. She also studied Creative Writing with poets Al Maginnes and Betty Adcock. Cays often draws poetry into her visual art through the use of whole poems, or word groupings. Her poems have been published in various small presses. She taught poetry writing while on the Board of Directors of The Arts Council, and taught drawing to students of varying ages, as well as to young adults who have Autism. She currently teaches workshops that intersect creative writing and visual arts as a personal narrative for people of all ages that focus on healing the human spirit.

Jane Chance, the Andrew W. Mellon Distinguished Professor Emerita in English at Rice University, received a D.litt. from Purdue University (2013). She has published twenty-three books on medieval literature and medievalism and been awarded Guggenheim and NEH Fellowships and a Bellagio residency, among other prizes. Her book of poems, *Only Begetter,* was published in 2014 and eight poems appeared in *New Crops From Old Fields: Eight Medievalist Poets,* ed. Oz Hardwick (2015). Her poems have also appeared in *Antigonish Review, Ariel, Dalhousie Review, Degenerates: Voices For Peace, Icarus* (Trinity College Dublin), *Ilanot Review, Kansas Quarterly, Literary Review, Lyric, New America, Nimrod, Poet Lore, Primavera, Quartet, Southern Humanities Review, Wascana Review,* as well as in the 2016 *Texas Poetry Calendar,* which nominated her poem "Enchanted Rock" for a Pushcart Prize. Selected as a Featured Poet by Houston Inprint First Fridays in 2013 and Juried Poet for the 2014-2015 Houston Poetry Festivals, she has studied under May Swenson and attended workshops with Marge Piercy, Gregory Pardlo, Kevin Young, Dorianne Laux and others.

Emily Rose Cole is a writer and lyricist from Pennsylvania. She has received awards from *Jabberwock Review, Ruminate Magazine, Winning Writers,* and the Academy of American Poets, and her poetry has appeared or is forthcoming in *Nimrod, Spoon River Poetry Review, Yemassee,* and *Passages North,* among others. She holds an MFA in poetry from Southern Illinois University Carbondale and is currently a PhD student at the University of Cincinnati.

Beth Copeland's second book *Transcendental Telemarketer* received the runner up award in the North Carolina Poetry Council's 2013 Oscar Arnold Young Award for best poetry book by a North Carolina writer. Her first book *Traveling through Glass* received the 1999 Bright Hill Press Poetry Book Award. Her poems have been published in various literary magazines and anthologies. This year she was profiled as poet of the week on the PBS NewsHour web site. An assistant professor of English at Methodist University in Fayetteville, she lives with her husband in a log cabin in rural North Carolina.

Heidi Czerwiec is a poet and essayist, and the poetry editor at *North Dakota Quarterly.* She is the author of two recent chapbooks — *A Is For A-ké, The Chinese Monster,* and *Sweet/Crude: A Bakken Boom Cycle* — and of the forthcoming collection *Maternal Imagination,* and is the editor of *North Dakota Is Everywhere: An Anthology of Contemporary North Dakota Poets.* She lives in Minneapolis. Her poem VII is excerpted from *Sweet/Crude: A Bakken Boom Cycle* (Gazing Grain Press) and also appears in literary journal *Eleven Eleven.*

Poet and visual artist **Carolyn Dahl** was the Grand Prize winner in the 2015 Public Poetry/MFAH ekphrastic poetry competition, ARTlines2. Her essays and poems have been published in anthologies including *Women On Poetry* (McFarland), *Goodbye, Mexico* (Texas Review Press), *Beyond Forgetting* (Kent State), and in various literary journals including *Copper Nickel, Camas, Hawaii Review, Colere, Sojourn,* and *Pirene's Fountain.* She is the co-author of the poetry and art book *The Painted Door Opened,* has received grants from the Texas Commission on the Arts, residencies to Hedgebrook and the Vermont Studio Center, and won a finalist award from PEN Texas in nonfiction.

Cortney Davis is the author of five poetry collections, including *Leopold's Maneuvers* (University of Nebraska Press, 2004), winner of the Prairie Schooner Poetry Book Prize and an American Journal of Nursing Book of the Year award. Her most recent non-fiction work is "When the Nurse Becomes a Patient: A Story in Words and Images." Her honors include an NEA Poetry Fellowship and three CT Commission on the Arts poetry grants. "In a Deep Pool Bound by Cement" previously appeared in *Leopold's Manuevers,* a volume that won the Prairie Schooner Book Prize in Poetry.

Lori Desrosiers' books are *The Philosopher's Daughter* (Salmon Poetry 2016), *Inner Sky* (a chapbook from Glass Lyre Press) and *Sometimes I Hear the Clock Speak* (new from Salmon Poetry). She edits *Naugatuck River Review,* a journal of narrative poetry, and WORDPEACE, an online journal dedicated to peace and justice. Her work has appeared in numerous journals, and she has been nominated for a Pushcart Prize. "After Leaving Him" was previously published in *Wingbeats: Exercises & Practices in Poetry* (edited by Scott Wiggerman & David Meischen, Dos Gatos Press, 2011).

Chelsea Dingman is a MFA candidate at the University of South Florida. In 2016, her work can be found in *Washington Square, The Normal School, Phoebe, American Literary Review, The Adroit Journal, Sou'wester,* and *Sugar House Review,* among others. She won the *Southeast Review's* Gearhart Poetry Contest (2016) and her first book, *Thaw,* where the poem in this anthology resides, has been a finalist in several contests. She is originally from Western Canada.

Ryler Dustin's poetry has appeared in *New South, Portland Review,* and elsewhere. He holds an MFA degree from the University of Houston and is a PhD in Poetry candidate at the University of Nebraska—Lincoln. He was a finalist in the Individual World Poetry Slam and his book, *Heavy Lead Birdsong,* is available from Write Bloody.

Dr. Angela "El Dia" Martinez Dy is a poet and writer, educator, community organiser, and hip-hop femmecee. An original member of isangmahal arts kollective, seminal in the millennial Asian American performance poetry movement, she co-founded Youth Speaks Seattle and helped it become a leading youth arts education organisation. Co-creator of Sisters of Resistance, a popular radical queer feminist blog (www.sistersofresistance.org), Angela recently attained her PhD on intersectionality and digital enterprise from Nottingham University. With her roots in Seattle and her heart in Manila, she is continually developing collaborative projects with an international network.

Rebecca Foust's most recent book, *Paradise Drive*, won the 2015 Press 53 Poetry Award and was reviewed in the *Georgia Review, Harvard Review, Hudson Review, Philadelphia Inquirer, San Francisco Chronicle, Washington Review of Books* and elsewhere. Recognitions include the 2015 American Literary Review Award for Fiction, the 2015 James Hearst Poetry Prize, the 2014 Constance Rook Creative Nonfiction Award, and fellowships from the Frost Place, MacDowell Colony, Sewanee Writer's Conference, and West Chester Poetry Conference "Sufferance" was previously published in *Bellingham Review*, 2015 and was a finalist for The 49th Parallel Award.

Joy Gaines-Friedler teaches advanced poetry and creative writing for non-profits in the Detroit area. Currently she is teaching male "lifer" inmates at The Thumb Correctional facility in LePeer, Mi. As best friends since 10th grade, Linda and Joy spoke with, or saw one another, every day. The morning of the night Linda's husband shot and killed her, Joy & Linda had had breakfast together. The next morning, Joy received a terrible phone call. Author of two books of poetry, a third manuscript completed, widely published in literary publications, nominated for a Pushcart Prize, Joy has dedicated her art to Linda. "After" was published in *Like Vapor* (Mayapple Press, 2008), and first appeared in *Swallow The Moon*, 2006.

Janice Moore Fuller has published four poetry collections, including *Séance* from Iris Press, winner of the 2008 Oscar Arnold Young Award (North Carolina poetry book of the year). Her most recent book, *On the Bevel*, was published in 2014 by Wales's Cinnamon Press. Her plays and libretti, including a stage adaptation of Faulkner's novel *As I Lay Dying*, have been produced at Catawba's Hedrick Theatre, BareBones Theater's New Play Festival, the Minneapolis Fringe Festival, Estonia's Polli Talu Centre, and France's Rendez-Vous Musique Nouvelle. Fuller is Writer-in-Residence, Professor of English, and the Weaver Endowed Chair of Humanities at Catawba College, where she has been awarded the Swink Prize for Outstanding Classroom Teacher and has been selected Professor of the Year five times by popular vote of the students. An Angier B. Duke Scholar at Duke University, she received her M.A. and Ph.D. from the University of North Carolina at Greensboro. "Excavation at Kampsville" was originally published in *Sex Education*, Iris Press, 2004.

Martha K. Grant is the author of *A Curse on the Fairest Joys* (Aldrich Press), poetry that explores the wounds of childhood and the blessings of healing. She has a Pushcart nomination and received an MFA in Poetry from Pacific University. Her work has has been published in *California Quarterly, New Texas, Earth's Daughters, The Yes! Book*, the anthology *Unruly Catholic Women Writers*, and nine editions of the *Texas Poetry Calendar*. A visual artist and a sixth generation Texan, she has a home and studio in the Hill Country northwest of San Antonio.

Jaki Shelton Green, the first NC Piedmont Laureate, has published numerous collections of poetry, including *Dead on Arrival, Conjure Blues, Masks, singing a tree into dance, breath of the song*, and *feeding the light*. Her work has appeared in such publications as *Ms., Essence*, and *The Crucible*. She is the recipient of the North Carolina Award for Literature, NC Literary Hall of Fame inductee, the Sam Ragan Award, and the Kathryn H. Wallace Award for Artists in Community Service. "brothers with dreadlocks will kill you too" is from *Feeding the Light* (Jacar Press 2014).

Chera Hammons is a graduate of the MFA in Creative Writing program at Goddard College. Her work has appeared in *Beloit Poetry Journal, Rattle, Tupelo Quarterly, Valparaiso Poetry Review*, and elsewhere. Her books include *Amaranthine Hour* (Jacar Press, 2012), *Recycled Explosions* (Ink Brush Press, 2016), and *The Traveler's Guide to Bomb City* (Purple Flag Press, forthcoming 2017). She is a winner of the 2016 Common Good Books Poetry Contest judged by Garrison Keillor. She lives in Amarillo, TX and serves as a member of the editorial board of poetry journal *One*, by Jacar Press.

Lois Marie Harrod's most recent collection *Nightmares of the Minor Poet* appears in June from Five Oaks. Her chapbook *And She Took the Heart* appeared in January 2016, and her 13th and 14th poetry collections, *Fragments from the Biography of Nemesis* (Cherry Grove Press) and the chapbook *How Marlene Mae Longs for Truth* (Dancing Girl Press) appeared in 2013. *The Only Is* won the 2012 Tennessee Chapbook Contest (Poems & Plays), and *Brief Term*, a collection of poems about teachers and teaching was published by Black Buzzard Press, 2011. *Cosmogony* won the 2010 Hazel Lipa Chapbook (Iowa State). She is widely published in literary journals and online ezines from *American Poetry Review* to *Zone 3*. She teaches Creative Writing at The College of New Jersey.

Melissa Hassard's poetry has been published in various journals such as *One*, by Jacar Press, the *North Dakota Quarterly, Vox Poetica*, and others. She was awarded the 2016 Thomas H. McDill Poetry Prize, honorary mention in the 2016 North Carolina Poet Laureate Award and the 2014 Randall Jarrell Poetry Competition. Melissa is partner and managing editor at Sable Books. "Dormitory" previously appeared in *North Dakota Quarterly*.

Joy Harold Helsing lives in the Sierra Nevada foothills of Northern California. Her work has appeared in many journals and she has published three chapbooks and one book, *Confessions of the Hare*. "Turnabout" was previously published in *Aftershocks: The Poetry of Recovery for Life-Shattering Events* (ed. Tom Lombardo, Sante Lucia Books, 2008).

Tony Hoagland's newest book of poems, *Application for Release from the Dream*, was just published by Graywolf Press in September. His most recent collections of essays about poetry is *Twenty Poems That Could Save America and Other Essays*, 2014, also from Graywolf. He teaches at the University of Houston. "The Roman Empire" first appeared in *Tin House* (the Tribes issue) and also appeared in *Application for Release from the Dream* (Graywolf Press, 2015).

Lizzie Holden is a London Poet who began writing poetry two years ago. Her wife died and in the space, the poetry poured in - one thousand poems, to date. She finds her poems are about abuse, trees, dance and breath; about love and loss and their sum: grief. Some of her poems are tiny, some can be found in *Pankhearst Press, Ealain, Tiger Shark Publishing, Picaroon Poetry* and *Kind of a Hurricane Press*.

Faith S. Holsaert has published fiction in journals since the 1980s and has begun to also publish poetry. She co-edited *Hands on the Freedom Plow: Personal Accounts by Women in SNCC* (University of Illinois). She received her mfa from the Warren Wilson Program for Writers. After many years in West Virginia, she lives in Durham, NC with her partner Vicki Smith, with whom she shares ten grandchildren.

Trish Hopkinson has always loved words—in fact, her mother tells everyone she was born with a pen in her hand. She has two chapbooks, *Emissions* and *Pieced Into Treetops*, and has been published in several anthologies and literary magazines, including *The Found Poetry Review, Chagrin River Review*, and *The Fem*. Trish is cofounder of a local poetry group, Rock Canyon Poets. Her poem, "A Leveling" was originally published in *Issue #2 Fall 2014*, Wicked Banshee Press, October 2014.

Kenan Ince is a mathematician from Dallas currently living in Salt Lake City. His work has appeared in *Word Riot* and *Permafrost*, among others, and has been ranted at in the comments section of the Houston real estate blog *Swamplot*. He has been featured in Houston's Poison Pen and Public Poetry reading series. He is the author of a chapbook entitled *Trickle-Down Theory*.

Elizabeth W. Jackson is a practicing psychologist who has published both essays and poems. Her poems have appeared in *Crab Orchard Review, Measure*, and *The Healing Muse* and in the anthologies *Intimacy* (Jacar Press) and *The Southern Poetry Anthology, Volume VII: North Carolina* (Texas A&M Univ Press). In 2014, she was awarded the James Applewhite Poetry Prize.

Alice-Catherine Jennings is the author of the chapbook *Katherine of Aragon: A Collection of Poems* published in 2016 by Finishing Line Press. Her poetry has appeared in numerous journals including *Hawai'i Review, Boyne Berries, GTK Creative, The Poets' Republic, First Literary Review East, The Louisville Review*, and *the quint:* an interdisciplinary quarterly from the north. She holds an MA in Slavic Languages and Literatures from The University of Texas at Austin and an MFA in Writing from Spalding University.

Edison Jennings is a part-time teacher and single father living in the western Appalachian region of Virginia. His poetry has appeared in a variety of journals and anthologies.

Sonja Johanson graduated from College of the Atlantic, in Bar Harbor, ME, is a contributing editor at the Found Poetry Review, and is the 2015 recipient of the Zero Bone and Kudzu Poetry Prizes. Her recent work can be found in *Albatross, Off the Coast,* and *Kudzu.* Sonja divides her time between work in Massachusetts and her home in the mountains of western Maine.

Quincy Scott Jones' work has appeared in publications such as the *African American Review, The North American Review,* and *The Feminist Wire,* as well the anthologies such as *Resisting Arrest: Poems to Stretch the Sky* and *Let Loose on the World: Celebrating Amiri Baraka at 75.* With Nina Sharma, he co-created the Nor'easter Exchange: a multicultural, multi-city reading series. His first book, *The T-Bone Series,* was published by Whirlwind Press in 2009.

Fady Joudah's poetry and translations have earned him a Yale Series of Younger Poets prize, a Guggenheim Fellowship, and the Griffin International Prize. His latest collections are *Alight* and *Textu.* "Hands" appears in *Alight* (Copper Canyon Press, 2013).

Athena Kashyap's second collection of poetry, *Sita's Choice,* is about women in India, and she has explored this topic deeply over the past five years. Her first collection, *Crossing Black Waters,* was a finalist for the SFA Awards, and published by them in 2012. She is currently living in India along with her husband and two daughters.

Debra Kaufman is the author of the poetry collections *Delicate Thefts, The Next Moment* (both by Jacar), and *A Certain Light* (Emrys), as well as three chapbooks. Her poems have appeared and are forthcoming in many magazines and anthologies, and her short plays have been widely produced. Her full-length play *Harbor Hope,* about domestic violence, was produced at Common Ground Theatre in Durham, NC, and at the NC Women's Theatre Festival. She is an editor for the online journal *One* and a member of the board of trustees of the Paul Green Foundation.

Loren Kleinman's poetry has appeared in journals such *ADAN-NA, Drunken Boat, The Moth, Domestic Cherry, Blue Lake Review, Catch & Release* (Columbia University), *LEVURE LITTÉRAIRE, Nimrod, Wilderness House Literary Review, Narrative Northeast, Writer's Bloc, Journal of New Jersey Poets, Paterson Literary Review (PLR), Resurgence* (UK), *HerCircleEzine* and *Aesthetica Annual.* Kleinman's *The Dark Cave Between My Ribs* was named one the best poetry book of 2014 by Entropy Magazine. Her third collection of poetry, *Breakable Things,* released via Winter Goose Publishing in March 2015. She is also working on a novel, *This Way to Forever,* a collection of prose poems, *Stay with Me Awhile,* and a memoir, *The Woman with a Million Hearts.* She is a faculty member at New York Writer's Workshop and a full-time freelance writer and social media strategist. "Stay with Me Awhile" appears in her collection by the same title, from Winter Goose Publishing, 2016.

Ellen Kombiyil is the author of *Histories of the Future Perfect* (2015), and the micro chapbook *Avalanche Tunnel* (Ryga, 2016). A fellow at the University of Iowa's International Writing Program (2013), and Sangam House (2013), she has new work forthcoming in *Boston Review, The Fiddlehead, The National Poetry Review* and *Prelude.* She has read, performed or taught workshops at Split This Rock, the Prakriti Poetry Festival in Chennai, the Raedleaf Poetry Awards in Hyderabad, and Lekhana in Bangalore, India. She is a co-Founder of The (Great) Indian Poetry Collective, a mentorship-model poetry press publishing emerging voices from India and the diaspora. She currently lives in New York City.

Richard Krawiec has published three books of poems, most recently *Women Who Loved Me Despite* (Press 53). His work appears in dozens of literary magazines, including *Drunken Boat, Shenandoah, sou'wester, Dublin Review, Blue Fifth Review, Chautauqua Literary Journal.* In addition to poetry, he has published two novels, a story collection, and four plays. He has been awarded fellowships from the National Endowment for the Arts, the NC Arts Council (twice), and the Pennsylvania Council on the Arts. He teaches online courses for the University of North Carolina at Chapel Hill, for which he won their Excellence in Teaching Award. He is founder of the literary magazine *One,* and Jacar Press, a community-active press. He has taught writing in homeless shelters, women's shelters, literacy classes, and Death Row at NC's Correctional Institute for Women.

Vishnupriya Krishnan is a a poet, yogi, musician, and outdoors-woman. As a member and Teaching Artist Assistant of the TOTUS Spoken Word Collective at the University of Maryland, she discovered her passion for using artistic efforts for social change. Her work has appeared in Write Bloody's anthology *We Will Be Shelter, Bethesda Magazine, Unbound Literary Magazine,* and *The Writer's Bloc.*

Gabrielle Langley has been featured in the *Huffington Post* as one of Houston's important emerging poets ("Five Poets You Need to Know About" from HuffPost 11/23/2015). A recipient of the Vivian Nellis Memorial Award for Creative Writing, an ARTlines national poetry finalist and a jury selected poet for Houston Poetry Fest (2015), her work has been appearing in a variety of literary journals in the United States and abroad. During the day, Ms. Langley works as a mental health professional. To safeguard her own mental health, she writes poetry and dances Argentine tango at night.

Jenna Le is a physician as well as the author of two poetry books, *Six Rivers* (NYQ Books, 2011) and *A History of the Cetacean American Diaspora* (Anchor & Plume Press, 2016). "Epitaph for a Young Woman" appears in *Six Rivers* (NYQ Books, 2011).

Stephanie Levin's collection *Smoke of Her Body* was chosen by Dorianne Laux as winner of Jacar Press's 2011 Poetry Book Prize. Her poems have appeared in *Green Mountains Review, Shenandoah, Prairie Schooner,* and elsewhere. She teaches writing through Johns Hopkins University's CTY*Online* and is one of the co-editors for *One,* Jacar Press's online poetry journal. She lives in Chapel Hill, NC with her two daughters.

Lisa Lewis's books include *The Unbeliever* (Brittingham Prize), *Silent Treatment* (National Poetry Series), *Vivisect* (New Issues Press), and *Burned House with Swimming Pool* (American Poetry Journal Prize, Dream Horse Press). A fifth volume, *The Body Double,* is newly released by Georgetown Review Press. New work appears in *Carolina Quarterly, Guernica, Sugar House Review, American Literary Review,* and elsewhere. She directs the creative writing program at Oklahoma State University and serves as poetry editor for the *Cimarron Review.*

Jessica Lohafer is a feminist poet out of Bellingham, WA, whose work has appeared in *Whatcom Magazine, The Noisy Water Review, Thriving Thru The Winter: A Pacific Northwest Handguide,* and *Drunk in the Midnight Choir.* Her collection of poetry, *What's Left to Be Done,* was published by Radical Lunchbox Press in 2009. She has served as the Program Director for Poetry in Public Education, bringing writing workshops to schools throughout the Pacific Northwest. Jessica recently received her MFA in poetry from Western Washington University. Currently, she works as the Chuckanut Writers Conference Planner. You can read her ongoing collection of poems and essays on her blog, *The Picture of Success.*

Ashley R. "Milli" Lumpkin is the author of two chapbooks, *{} At First Sight* and *Terrorism and Other Topics for Tea*. A lover of performance as well as the written word, she has been a competing member of Piedmont SLAM, Scuppernong Slammers, and the Bull City Slam team. Ashley has been a featured presenter and/or facilitator at various colleges and universities, including: Elon University, Davidson College, North Carolina A&T State University, UNC Wilmington, Bennett College, Hampton University, and Rutgers University. Above all else, Ashley considers herself a teacher, poet, and fryer of food. She is a lover of mathematics and language. She loves you too.

Cecile Lusby's mature life began with divorce and single motherhood, finishing her education in midlife. She earned her credentials as an English teacher and a school counselor working with teenage foster youth in San Mateo County. She is retired and lives in Sonoma County where she volunteers for the Interchurch Pantry of Sebastopol and contributes to the *Sonoma County Gazette* and the *Independent Coast Review*.

Djelloul Marbrook is working on a collection of poems about sexual predation of children. His first book of poetry, *Far From Algiers,* won the Stan and Tom Wick Poetry Prize in 2007. It was followed by three more volumes of poetry. A fifth collection, *Riding Thermals to Winter Grounds,* will be published by Leaky Boot Press, UK, in November 2016. Two books of fiction are also in production, *Making Room,* a novella an short stories set in Baltimore, and *A Warding Circle,* a novella and short stories set in New York City and the Hudson Valley.

David Tomas Martinez's debut collection of poetry, *Hustle,* was released in 2014 by Sarabande Books, winning the New England Book Festival's prize in poetry, the Devil's Kitchen Reading Award, and honorable mention in the Antonio Cisneros Del Moral Prize. He is the 2015 winner of the Verlaine Poetry Prize from Inprint. Martinez is a Pushcart winner, CantoMundo fellow, and a recipient of the Stanley P. Young Fellowship from Broadleaf. A second collection is forthcoming from Sarabande Books. "Shed" first appeared in *Hustle.*

Carmel Mawle is the founder of Writing for Peace and editor of *DoveTales,* an International Journal of the Arts. Mawle has a varied career that includes piano instruction, women and children's self-defense, as well as and traditional Hayashi-Ha Shito Ryu Karate and Kobudo (weapons) training. Mawle has served as executive director of a youth orchestra, and as president of a chamber music organization. Mawle's work has appeared in *Smokelong Quarterly Review, KNOT Magazine, SPACES Literary Magazine, Lucid Moose's "Like A Girl" Anthology, Mom Egg Review, Shake The Tree Anthology, When Women Waken,* and is forthcoming in Coda Crab Book's anthology, *Peace: Give it a Chance.*

Marty McConnell lives in Chicago, Illinois, where she coaches individuals and groups toward building thriving, sustainable lives and organizations. An MFA graduate of Sarah Lawrence College, her work has recently appeared in *Best American Poetry 2014, Southern Humanities Review, Gulf Coast,* and *Indiana Review,* and is forthcoming in *Southampton Poetry Review.* Her first full-length collection, *wine for a shotgun,* was published by EM Press.

Addy Robinson McCulloch was a finalist for the 2014 Fairy Tale Review inaugural poetry contest and received a Best of the Net nomination from *vox poetica* in 2014. Her work has appeared or is forthcoming in publications such as *Minerva Rising; Gingerbread House; Redheaded Stepchild; the Iodine Review; What Matters,* an anthology of poetry from Jacar Press; and *Get Out of My Crotch: 21 Writers Respond to America's War on Women's Rights and Reproductive Health.* Addy is a graduate of Duke University and a freelance writer and editor.

Seth Michelson's collections of poetry include *Swimming through Fire, Eyes Like Broken Windows, House in a Hurricane, Kaddish for My Unborn Son,* and *Maestro of Brutal Splendor.* His translations of poetry include the books *The Ghetto* (Tamara Kamenszain, Argentina), *roly poly* (Victoria Estol, Uruguay), *Poems from the Disaster* (Zulema Moret, Argentina/Spain), and *Dreaming in Another Land* (Rati Saxena, India). He currently teaches the poetry of the Americas at Washington and Lee University, as well as in a high-security prison for undocumented, unaccompanied youth. "Manifesto" was previously published in *Eyes Like Broken Windows* (Press 53, 2012).

Denise Miller is a professor, poet and mixed media artist whose work reflects the necessity for conscious survival for individuals living in an "ism" driven culture. She's a Willow Books Emerging Poet, an AROHO Waves Discussion Fellowship awardee, a finalist for the Barbara Deming Money for Women Fund and a Hedgebrook Fellow. Her book, *Core,* has just been released from Willow Books. Most recently, one of her poems has been nominated for the Pushcart Prize. She also facilitates the project s.t.e.p. (speaking truth equals power), a series of workshops that focuses on the power to tell our own stories, that brings together artist-survivors from traditionally marginalized groups (people of color, abuse and sexual assault survivors, queer and trans identified people and women) to "speak" about their experiences of violence against their bodies through conventional dialogue, movement, writing, art, film, photography, performance, and voice.

Tracy Mishkin is a call center veteran with a PhD and an MFA student in Creative Writing at Butler University. Her chapbook, *I Almost Didn't Make It to McDonald's*, was published by Finishing Line Press in 2014. Her work has appeared in *Rat's Ass Review, Little Patuxent Review,* and *Postcard Poems and Prose.*

Thylias Moss, a self-employed multi-racial "maker" at Thylias Moss Writing LLC, is also Professor Emerita in the Departments of English and Art & Design at the University of Michigan. Author of ten published books, and recipient of numerous awards and honors, among them a MacArthur Fellowship, and a Guggenheim Fellowship. Her 11th book, a collection of New & Selected Poetry, *Wannabe Hoochie Mama Gallery of Realities' Red Dress Code* (from Persea Books, September 2016) links to a video poam she made for her YouTube channel, where many poams (product[s] of act[s] of making) are displayed as part of Limited Fork Theory, an approach to making and thinking developed in order to assist co-makers and co-learners become more collaborative in thinking and being. All about how things interact across all boundaries, and encouragement of interaction that becomes more meaningful over time; all have collaborators. Nothing makes alone, and there is nothing that exists that does not make stuff in some form, which is also open: any form that becomes possible; invent whenever necessary. "Making" is not static, is evidence of life, as is the romance novel on which she works, soon to be book #12. "In the Time of Scurvy" is from an unpublished collection: *LFMK: Looking for my Killer,* an act of public service (while my killer is attacking me, he cannot be attacking you).

Kathleen Nalley is the author of *Nesting Doll* (winner of the S.C. Poetry Initiative Prize), and *American Sycamore* (Finishing Line Press). Her poetry is forthcoming or has recently appeared in *New Flash Fiction Review, Slipstream, Rivet, storySouth, Night Block, The Bitter Southerner, Melancholy Hyperbole,* and *Night Owl,* among others. She holds an MFA from Converse College, teaches literature and writing at Clemson University, and finds books their forever homes at M. Judson Books.

Stacy R. Nigliazzo's debut poetry collection *Scissored Moon* was published in 2013 by Press 53. It was awarded Book of the Year by the American Journal of Nursing and named a finalist for the Julie Suk Poetry Prize (Jacar Press) and the Texas Institute of Letters First Book Award for Poetry/Bob Bush Award. She serves as a reviewer for the *Bellevue Literary Review.* (srnigliazzo.com) "Triptych (for Caroline)" originally appeared in the *Lumen Blog,* 2015.

Ashley Nissler's work has been published in *Cricket, Ladybug, Strange Horizons, Tar River Poetry, Literary Mama, poemeleon, The Black Boot, Vestal Review, The Mom Egg, BLIP* (now *New World Writing*), *Dogzplot,* and *Nailpolish Stories.* In addition to her story "Lungs once pink and fragile" being nominated for a Pushcart Prize, she received an Emerging Artist's Grant from the Durham Arts Council in 2005.

Naomi Shihab Nye's most recent books are *Famous* (Wings Press 2015) and *The Turtle of Oman* (Greenwillow 2014, just out in paperback). An earlier version of her poem "Everything Changes the World" first appeared in *Sojourners* (November, 2014).

Katherine Durham Oldmixon's recent poems can be found in *Borderlands: Texas Poetry Review, Solstice Literary Magazine, The Bellevue Review, The Normal School,* and in her chapbook *Water Signs,* finalist for the New Women's Voices Award (Finishing Line Press, 2009). Katherine co-directs the Poetry at Round Top festival and is a senior poetry editor for *Tupelo Quarterly.* She is professor and chair of English at historic Huston-Tillotson University in Austin, TX, where she lives with her husband Arturo Lomas Garza.

Linda Parsons is an editor at the University of Tennessee. She served as poetry editor of *Now & Then* magazine for many years, and her work has appeared in such journals as *The Georgia Review, Iowa Review, Prairie Schooner, Southern Poetry Review,* and *Shenandoah.* Her fourth poetry collection, *This Shaky Earth,* is forthcoming from Texas Review Press. Her new play, *Macbeth Is the New Black,* co-written with Jayne Morgan, will be produced at Western Carolina University in early 2016. "My Stepmother Takes Me to the Fair" was originally published in her second book, *Mother Land* (Iris Press, 2008).

Artist and poet **Rebecca Pierre** has been writing poetry for more than 25 years. Her poetry has appeared in *Asheville Poetry Review, Wellspring, Cancer Poetry Project I & II, The Peralta Press, Lullwater Review, NCPS Pinesong Awards, Illya's Honey, Of Frogs and Toads,* and *Literary Trails of NC* among others. "The Gun" originally appeared in *Asheville Poetry Review.*

Deborah Pope is the author of three poetry collections—*Fanatic Heart, Mortal World* and *Falling Out of the Sky.* She has been nominated for the National Book Award, the Walt Whitman Award and for the Pushcart Prize. Her work has appeared in *Poetry, Threepenny Review, Michigan Quarterly, Southern Review, TriQuarterly, The Georgia Review, Poetry Northwest, Southwest Quarterly, Prairie Schooner, Tar River Poetry,* among others. She is on the English faculty at Duke University.

Kevin Prufer is the author of several books of poetry, most recently *National Anthem* (Four Way Books, 2008), *In a Beautiful Country* (Four Way Books, 2011) and *Churches* (Four Way Books, 2014). He's also editor of numerous volumes, including *New European Poets* (Graywolf, 2008; w/Wayne Miller) and *Into English: Essays on Multiple Translations* (Graywolf, 2016; w/Martha Collins). He is Professor of English in the Creative Writing Program at the University of Houston. "The Man in Miami" appears in *Strange Wood* (Winthrop/LSU, 1997).

Writer, teacher, and clarinetist **Ann Quinn** lives in Catonsville, Maryland with her family, and is working towards an M.F.A. in poetry with the Rainier Writing Workshop at Pacific Lutheran University. She won first prize in the 2015 Bethesda Literary Festival Poetry Contest, judged by Stanley Plumly and has been a Pushcart Prize nominee.

Molly Pershin Raynor founded RAW Talent which recently merged with the RYSE Center in Richmond, California, to become its Performing Arts Program. Through the lens of spoken word poetry and theater, the program provides workshops, field trips, performance and publication opportunities to over 100 Richmond youth each year. Her work is highlighted in the documentary film, "Romeo Is Bleeding", which follows her staff and students as they fight to address local turf violence through spoken word and theater. Molly is a poet and educator. She has facilitated creative writing workshops in prisons, halfway houses, high schools, teen centers and summer camps and has traveled from coast to coast performing spoken word and organizing youth slams. She's published two poetry chapbooks and has been featured on National Public Radio.

Maria Rouphall is the author of the chapbook, *Apertures,* a 2012 finalist in Finishing Line Press's "New Women's Voices" competition. *Second Skin,* her second collection of poems, was published in the Fall, 2015, by Main Street Rag. Her poem, "Crater at Popocatepetl," won Honorable Mention in the 2016 Randall Jarrel Poetry Competition. She is currently at work on her third poetry collection.

Carly Sachs is the author of *the steam sequence* and the editor of *the why and later,* a collection of poems about rape and assault. Her poems and stories have been published near and far and included in *The Best American Poetry* series and read on NPR's Selected Shorts. Carly also holds a 500-hour Kripalu yoga certification, with additional certifications in restorative and trauma-informed yoga.

Metta Sáma is author of the chapbooks *the year we turned dragon* (Portable Press @ Yo-Yo Labs), *le animal and other creatures* (Miel), *After After/After "Sleeping to Dream"* (Nous-zot Press), and *Nocturne Trio* (Yes Yes Books). Her poems, fiction, creative non-fiction, literary scholarship & book reviews have been published in various literary journals and anthologies. Co-winner of the Poetry Society of Award 2016 Robert H. Winner Memorial Award, Sáma is a Black Earth Institute fellow, a member of the Cave Canem Board, and the Advisory Board of Black Radish Books.

Judy Schaefer, RN, MA, whose most recent book is *Wild Onion Nurse* (Radcliffe, 2010), edited the first biographical/ autobiographical work of English speaking nurse-poets, *The Poetry* *of Nursing: Poems and Commentaries of Leading Nurse-Poets* (Kent State University Press, 2006), and co-edited the first international anthology of creative writing by nurses, *Between the Heartbeats* (University of Iowa Press, 1995). She has been published in journals such as *Academic Medicine, The American Journal of Nursing* and *The Lancet.* She is a poetry editor for *Pulse: voices from the heart of medicine* (www.pulsevoices.org). Her poem, "Peacemongering," was previously published in *Wild Onion Nurse* (Radcliffe, 2010) and first published in *Wild Onions* (Penn State University College of Medicine, 2009).

Penelope Scambly Schott is the author of a novel, ten full-length poetry books, and six chapbooks. Her verse biography *A is for Anne: Mistress Hutchinson Disturbs the Commonwealth* won an Oregon Book Award for Poetry. Recent books include *Lovesong for Dufur* and *Lillie Was a Goddess, Lillie Was a Whore. How I Became an Historian* was Published in 2014. Penelope lives in Portland and Dufur, Oregon where she teaches a notorious poetry workshop. "Gleaner" appears in *How I Became an Historian* (Cherry Grove Collections, 2015).

Rebecca Seiferle is a poet, editor, teacher and translator, who since arriving in Tucson in 2006 has played an important role in the literary arts at the local, national and international levels. In addition to being awarded a Lannan Foundation Poetry Fellowship in 2004, Seiferle's four poetry collections have received national prizes, among them the Grub Street National Poetry Prize, Western States Book Award, two awards from the Poetry Society of America and an award each from Poets & Writers and the National Writers' Union. Her last three publications have been nominated for Pulitzer Prizes. She is editor at *Drunken Boat.* She also has regularly reviewed for the *Harvard Review* and *Calyx.* "The Voices of Women" has previously appeared in *Blue Fifth Review.*

B.T. Shaw earned a bachelor of science degree in journalism from University of Oregon and a master of fine arts from University of Washington. Her work has received support from Oregon Literary Arts and the National Endowment for the Art. Her first collection, *This Dirty Little Heart,* won the 2007 Blue Lynx Poetry Prize. A collection of found poems, *Shake it up & throw it at something hard,* was published online by Essay Press in 2016. She lives in Jakarta, Indonesia.

Shoshauna Shy's poetry has been included in anthologies by Marion Street Press, Random House, Midmarch Arts Press, Grayson Books, Ragged Sky, Dos Gatos Press and others. She is the author of four collections of poetry; the most recent one titled *What the Postcard Didn't Say* won an Outstanding Achievement Poetry Award from the Wisconsin Library Association. Her poetry has recently been published by *IthacaLit, Red Cedar, Hartskill Review, RHINO* and *Sliver of Stone.*

Sue William Silverman's poetry collection, *Hieroglyphics in Neon,* was published by Orhises Press. She is also the author of four non-fiction books. *The Pat Boone Fan Club: My Life as a White Anglo-Saxon Jew* is part of the American Lives Series with the University of Nebraska Press. *Because I Remember Terror, Father, I Remember You* won the Association of Writers and Writing Programs award in creative nonfiction. *Love Sick: One Woman's Journey through Sexual Addiction,* published with W. W. Norton, is also a Lifetime TV movie, and her craft book is *Fearless Confessions: A Writer's Guide to Memoir.* She teaches in the MFA in Writing Program at Vermont College of Fine Arts.

Marty Silverthorne resides in Greenville, North Carolina, where he is a licensed Clinical Addiction Specialist. He holds degrees from St. Andrews Presbyterian College and East Carolina University. His collections of poems are *Dry-Skin Messiah, Pot Liquor Promises, No Welfare, No Pension Plan,* and *Rewinding at 40.* He was the recipient of the Sam Ragan Award 1993 and has received several NC Arts Regional Grants. "Tongue and Groove" appears in his chapbook-length collection, *Holy Ghosts of Whiskey* (Sable Books 2015).

Sharon Sitler lives in Western Massachusetts with her adorable and witty young son, two rabbits, and a slightly insane cat. She graduated from Westfield State University with a BA in English Literature and currently teaches high school writing and literature at a special education day school. Her poetry has appeared in *Fresh Ink, Prairie Margins, Paper Nautilus,* and *Big River Poetry Review.*

Karen Skolfield's book *Frost in the Low Areas* (Zone 3 Press) won the 2014 PEN New England Award in poetry. She received fellowships and awards in 2014/2015 from the Poetry Society of America, New England Public Radio, the Massachusetts Cultural Council, Ucross Foundation, Split This Rock, Hedgebrook, and Vermont Studio Center. New poems appear in Crab Orchard Review, Crazyhorse, Guernica, Indiana Review, Pleiades, and others; she teaches writing to engineers at the University of Massachusetts Amherst. "Two Sisters" first appeared in *Linebreak.*

Andrea Witzke Slot is winner of *Able Muse* and *Fiction International's* 2015 Prizes in Fiction, with her winning work described by Eugenia Kim as having "a rare and satisfying command of storytelling" and by Harold Jaffe as "meld[ing] compression, humor, keen intelligence, and social awareness." She is author of the poetry collection *To find a new beauty* (Gold Wake Press, 2012) and a recently-finished novel titled *The Cartography of Flesh: in the silence of Ella Mendelssohn.* Recent poetry and fiction can be found in such places as *Nimrod, Fiction Southeast, The American Literary Review, Bellevue Literary Review, Meridian, Tupelo Quarterly, Southeast Review,* and in the anthology *All We Can Hold: poems of motherhood* (Sage Hill Press, 2016). Her essays on the university faculty crisis can be found in *The Chronicle* *of Higher Education* while her academic papers on poetry and social change can be found in books published by SUNY Press (2013) and Palgrave Macmillan (2014). After teaching for a number of years (primary school level in England and college/university level in the U.S. after receiving her PhD), Andrea now writes full-time. She is mother/stepmother to five children and calls both London and Chicago home.

Aleenah Spencer is currently striving for patience and positivity. Aleenah is currently in graduate school at Texas A&M University working on receiving her Master's in Biomedical Sciences. In the future she is looking to pursue her Doctorates in Veterinary Medicine. Presently, she is just trying to stay balanced in the sciences and the arts.

Alison Stone is the author of five poetry collections, including *Ordinary Magic,* (NYQ Books,2016), *Dangerous Enough* (Presa Press 2014), and *They Sing at Midnight,* which won the 2003 Many Mountains Moving Poetry Award and was published by Many Mountains Moving Press. Her poems have appeared in *The Paris Review, Poetry, Ploughshares, Barrow Street, Poet Lore,* and a variety of other journals and anthologies. She has been awarded *Poetry's* Frederick Bock Prize and *New York Quarterly's* Madeline Sadin award. She is also a painter and the creator of The Stone Tarot. A licensed psychotherapist, she has private practices in NYC and Nyack. She is currently editing an anthology of poems on the Persephone/Demeter myth.

Melissa Studdard is host of VIDA *Voices & Views* and an editor for *American Microreviews and Interviews.* She is the author of the novel, *Six Weeks to Yehidah,* a poetry collection, *I Ate the Cosmos for Breakfast,* and a collection of interviews, *The Tiferet Talk Interviews.* Her awards include the Forward National Literature Award and the International Book Award, among others. Of her debut poetry collection, *I Ate the Cosmos for Breakfast,* Robert Pinsky writes, "This poet's ardent, winning ebullience echoes that of God..." and Cate Marvin says her work "would have no doubt pleased Neruda's taste for the alchemic impurity of poetry." "For the Women of Atenco" was originally published in *Hip Poetry 2012* Anthology (Wind Publications, February 2012).

Leslie Waugh is a yoga teacher and journalist. She worked as a copy editor at the Kinston Free Press, the Raleigh News & Observer and the Washington Post. She now works part time for the Post's editorial department and has also copy-edited novels and nonfiction books. Her writing has been published in the Smithsonian magazine blog and the Post. Her poem "Running for My Life" received an honorable mention in *Carolina Woman* magazine's 2015 writing contest, and "Why I Stayed" appeared in the Fall 2015 edition of the journal *When Women Waken.* She attends writing workshops to make up for the English degree road not taken, and she also loves photography. She lives in Clayton, N.C., with her husband and is pursuing a 2,000-hour certification in Purna Yoga.

LaWanda Walters grew up in Mississippi and North Carolina and received an M.F.A. in Poetry from Indiana University, where she won the Academy of American Poets Prize. Her poems have appeared in *The Antioch Review, The Cincinnati Review, Cutthroat, The Georgia Review, The Laurel Review, North American Review, Ploughshares, Shenandoah, Southern Poetry Review,* and *Sou'wester.* Her poem "Marilyn Monroe" appears in *Obsession: Sestinas in the Twenty-First Century* (Dartmouth College Press, 2014). "Goodness in Mississippi" was chosen by Sherman Alexie for *Best American Poetry 2015.* She is the mother of two grown children, Tess Despres Weinberg and Sean Jason Weinberg, and lives with her husband, John Philip Drury, in Cincinnati. "First Marriage" was first published in *Light Is the Odalisque* (Press 53, 2016).

Monica Wendel is the author of *No Apocalypse,* which was selected by Bob Hicok as the winner of the Georgetown Review Press poetry manuscript prize. She is also the author of three chapbooks, most recently *English Kills* (Autumn House Press, 2016). Her work has appeared in *Rattle, Ploughshares, Forklift Ohio,* and other journals.

Chris Wise is a poet and novelist. He has been published in various poetry anthologies and small press literary magazines such as *Nerve Cowboy, Blue Collar Review,* and *Road Not Taken.* He has been a featured author in *Cowboys and Indians Magazine* and has made several radio appearances on KPFT's *Living Art,* Houston Public Poetry, and the Word Around Town Poetry Tour. His book *Colliding With Orion Writing From Life* (a collection of poetry, short stories and essays on craft) from Absey & Co. will be released in the fall of 2016. He is a veteran of the US Army, earned an English degree from Texas A&M, and currently lives in Houston, TX.

Laura Madeline Wiseman is the author of twenty books and chapbooks, including *Drink* (BlazeVOX Books, 2015) and *Wake* (Aldrich Press, 2015).

Andy Young is a poet and essayist. Her poem "Fire on the Prophet's Face" appears in *All Night It Is Morning,* published in 2014 by Diálogos Press. She teaches at New Orleans Center for Creative Arts and is a writer for Heinemann Publishing. Her work has appeared in places such as *Los Angeles Review of Books, Guernica, New World Writing,* and *One,* as well as in electronic and flamenco music and as elements in visual art.

Katherine E. Young is the author of *Day of the Border Guards,* 2014 Miller Williams Arkansas Poetry Prize finalist (University of Arkansas Press), and translator of *Two Poems by Inna Kabysh* (Artist's Proof Editions). Her poems appear in *Prairie Schooner, The Iowa Review, Shenandoah,* and others. Her translations of Russian poets Xenia Emelyanova and Inna Kabysh won third prize in the Joseph Brodsky-Stephen Spender competitions in 2014 and 2011, respectively. In 2016, she was named the inaugural Poet Laureate of Arlington, VA.

Proceeds raised from the sale of this book
will go to the Global Fund for Women.